Encyclopaedia of Eminent Thinkers Series

Vol. I. The Political Thought of Mahatma Gandhi/ *K.S. Bharti*
Vol. II. The Political Thought of Nehru/ *K.S. Bharti*
Vol. III. The Political Thought of Rabindra Nath Tagore/ *K.S. Bharti*
Vol. IV. The Political Thought of Radhakrishnan/ *K.S. Bharti*
Vol. V. The Political Thought of Vinoba/ *K.S. Bharti*
Vol. VI. The Political Thought of Aurobindo/ *K.S. Bharti*
Vol. VII. The Political Thought of Jayaprakash Narayan/ *K.S. Bharti*
Vol. VIII. The Political Thought of Vivekananda/ *K.S. Bharti*
Vol. IX. The Political Thought of Ambedkar/ *K.S. Bharti*
Vol. X. The Political Thought of M.N. Roy/ *K.S. Bharti*
Vol. XI. The Political Thought of Dadabhai Naoroji/ *Ashu Pasricha*
Vol. XII. The Political Thought of Veer Savarkar/ *Jai Narain Sharma*
Vol. XIII. The Political Thought of M.A. Jinnah/ *Jai Narain Sharma*
Vol. XIV. The Political Thought of Tej Bahadur Sapru/ *Ashu Pasricha*
Vol. XV. The Political Thought of C. Rajagopalachari/ *Ashu Pasricha*
Vol. XVI. The Political Thought of Subhas Chandra Bose/ *Ashu Pasricha*
Vol. XVII. The Political Thought of Mohammad Iqbal/ *Jai Narain Sharma*
Vol. XVIII. The Political Thought of K.B. Hedgewar/ *Jai Narain Sharma*
Vol. XIX. The Political Thought of Bhagat Singh/ *Ashu Pasricha*
Vol. XX. The Political Thought of M.S. Golwalkar/ *Jai Narain Sharma*
Vol. XXI. The Political Thought of Sir Syed Ahmed Khan/ *Jai Narain Sharma*
Vol. XXII. The Political Thought of Mahadev Govind Ranade/ *Ashu Pasricha*
Vol. XXIII. The Political Thought of Pandit Deendayal Upadhyaya/ *Jai Narain Sharma*
Vol. XXIV. The Political Thought of Lokmanya Bal Gangadhar Tilak/ *Jai Narain Sharma*
Vol. XXV. The Political Thought of Annie Besant/ *Ashu Pasricha*

Forthcoming

The Political Thought of C.R. Das/ *Ashu Pasricha*
The Political Thought of Gopal Krishna Gokhale/ *Jai Narain Sharma*
The Political Thought of Lala Lajpat Rai/ *Ashu Pasricha*
The Political Thought of Maulana Abul Kalam Azad/ *Jai Narain Sharma*
The Political Thought of Sir Pherozeshah Mehta/ *Ashu Pasricha*

CONTENTS

souls in all the lands, and not merely on account of his intellectual power, his learning or patriotism. It is true that these virtues are so rare that many could have earned a world-wide reputation on account of anyone of them; but he was endowed with an even rarer attitude of mind. Such an attitude is not to be found but in the greatest of saints. This saintly attitude of Ranade manifested itself in a full growth of refined attributes and these convinced one of the essential divinity of Raosahib's personality. Had he been born a few centuries earlier, he would surely have been counted among the divine incarnations.

With this perspective in mind in the present work, an attempt has been made to discuss the political ideas of Justice Ranade.

Personal acknowledgements are no easy matters where so many have been kind. My special thanks are due to Professor R.N. Pal, Professor N. Radhakrishnan, Dr. K.S. Bharathi, Dr. A.D. Mishra, Professor Jai Narain Sharma, Dr. Meena Dutta, Dr. Seema Pasricha, Dr. Rashmi Sharma, Mr. Ajay Pasricha (Advocate) and Master Hemant Malhotra. Beyond that I can make only an all embracing salute to the galaxy of the scholars whose works I have consulted.

I am also grateful to Shri Ashok Kumar Mittal, my publisher, for his consistent zeal in the printing and publication of this volume.

Chandigarh **ASHU PASRICHA**

PREFACE

Justice Mahadev Govind Ranade (1842-1901) was one of the greatest and most representative Indians of his time. He was an erudite scholar, a profound thinker, a devoted patriot, and a distinguished official. In the last quarter of the nineteenth century, India was passing through a social and cultural ferment. Men emerging from the newly started universities became conscious of national degeneration, and several of them were eager to transform the country in all aspects of its life: religious, cultural, social, economic and political. It was this eagerness for all-sided reform of society which Ranade represented in the fullest measure. His splendid talents, his unrivalled attainments, his learning, his scholarship, his balanced mind, his clear judgement, his capacity for comprehensive views, his indomitable energy and his indefatigable industry marked him out as a leader of men; while his high character, his absolute honesty of purpose, his boundless patriotism, his lofty ideals, his moderation, his patience, and his exalted sense of duty—which never swerved from its task and knew no aim—save that of serving his country, inspired confidence and won for him the enthusiastic attachment and devotion of his fellow-workers and followers.

His broad, comprehensive and brilliant intellectual power, his profound knowledge, gigantic industry and ethereal magnetism were all dedicated to the loyal service of the country. No other thoughts ever touched his mind but those of how this land of the Aryas could be rendered beautiful in all aspects, how it could progress step by step in all respects—social, political, religious, moral, industrial or educational—and how the men and women in our community could acquire all the qualities necessary for such progress. Such patriotism and such faith in efforts for the uplift of a nation are rare indeed, in any country. But, Ranade is to be counted among the greatest

DEDICATED
TO
ADVOCATE RAMESH CHANDRA MEHTA
AND
SHRIMATI USHA MEHTA

Cataloging in Publication Data—DK
Courtesy: D.K. Agencies (P) Ltd. docinfo@dkagencies.com

Encyclopaedia of eminent thinkers.
p. cm. — (Gandhian studies and peace research series : 11)
Vols. 11- lack series statement.
In Indian context.
Includes bibliographical references.
Includes indexes.
Contents: v. 22 The political thought of Mahadev Govind Ranade / Ashu Pasricha.
ISBN 13: 9788180695827
ISBN 10: 8180695824

1. Statesmen—India. 2. Political science—India. 3. India—Politics and government. I. Sharma, Jai Narain, 1951- II. Pasricha, ashu, 1967- III. Series: Gandhian studies and peace research series ; 11.

DDC 954.035 22

ISBN-13: 978-81-7022-684-0 (Series)
ISBN-10: 81-7022-684-8 (Series)
ISBN-13: 978-81-8069-582-7 (Vol. XXII)
ISBN-10: 81-8069-582-4 (Vol. XXII)

First Published 2009

Published and Printed by
Ashok Kumar Mittal
Concept Publishing Company
A/15-16, Commercial Block, Mohan Garden
New Delhi-110059 (India)

Phones: 25351460, 25351794
Fax: 091-11-25357103
E-mail: publishing@conceptpub.com

ENCYCLOPAEDIA OF EMINENT THINKERS

VOLUME-TWENTY TWO

THE POLITICAL THOUGHT OF MAHADEV GOVIND RANADE

Dr. Ashu Pasricha
Department of Gandhian Studies
Panjab University
Chandigarh

CONCEPT PUBLISHING COMPANY, NEW DELHI-110059

Volumes by the same author

The Political Thought of ***Dadabhai Naoroji***
The Political Thought of ***Tej Bahadur Sapru***
The Political Thought of ***C. Rajagopalachari***
The Political Thought of ***Subhas Chandra Bose***
The Political Thought of ***Bhagat Singh***
The Political Thought of ***Annie Besant***
The Political Thought of ***C.R. Das***
The Political Thought of ***Lala Lajpat Rai***
The Political Thought of ***Sir Pherozeshah Mehta***
The Political Thought of ***Mahadev Govind Ranade***

About the Author

Dr. (Miss) Ashu Pasricha is a faculty in Gandhian studies at Panjab University, Chandigarh. She has many books to her credit including *Gandhian Approach to Integrated Rural Development; Public Administration: Discipline and Dimensions; Peace Studies: Discipline and Dimensions; WTO, Self-reliance and Globalisation; and Gandhi's Concept of State and Power.* Also, she has published a number of research papers in various Indian and foreign journals of repute.

ENCYCLOPAEDIA OF EMINENT THINKERS

VOLUME-XXII: **MAHADEV GOVIND RANADE**

1

LIFE AND HIS ACTIVITIES

The Ranades came from a family belonging to the Chitpavan Brahmin community, which originally lived in the narrow strip between the Sahyadri ranges and the Arabian Sea, known as Konkan. For thousands of years, the Chitpavans lived modestly and inconspicuously in Konkan, performing their priestly functions and eking out from relatively infertile soil the bare necessities of life. With the foundation of Shivaji's power in Maharashtra, there began some migration from Konkan to his kingdom, but it was inconsiderable. However, one incident at the end of the seventeenth century gave a new turn to the history of the community. A part of Konkan, Shrivardhan, was under an Abbysinian Muslim ruler, the Siddi of Janjira; and one of the Chitpavans Janoji Vishwanath, functioned as the Deshmukh of the region. The Marathas had all along been at war with this ruler; and Sardar Angre succeeded in winning over this Deshmukh to their side. When the Siddi came to know of this, he was all fury. He swooped upon Janoji, put him into a sack, sewed the sack tight on all sides, and threw it deep into the sea. Janoji's brother Balaji Vishwanath, together with a friend, who lived in a neighbouring village, ran for his life, crossed the mountain, reached Satara, and obtained a modest job with the Marathas, then fighting for survival. Subsequently, he won the confidence of King Sahu who came to the throne in 1708. By dint of his ability as an administrator, politician and warrior, he rose in service till he became the Peshwa or the Chief Minister. His son, Bajirao I, was appointed to succeed him. Bajirao proved himself to be so able that he and his successors became *de facto* rulers of the Maratha kingdom. These examples provided an inspiration to others in Konkan; moreover, they could now expect patronage from the administration. During the Peshwa regime, and especially during the latter half of the eighteenth century, the migration of Chitpavans from Konkan to the Deccan plateau became common. New opportunities, afforded first by the Peshwa and later by the British rule, revealed qualities which till then had lain dormant; and the Chitpavan community till this day has been throwing up men of extraordinary intellect, industry and perseverance in a remarkably large number. A little after the middle of the eighteenth century, following the trend of the times, a Chitpavan from the village Mobharpacheri or Pacherisada in the Chiplun taluk of the Ratnagiri district, by name Bhagwantrao Ranade, left Konkan for the east in the hope of improving his fortune in the more prosperous land. He began to live in Karkamb near Pandharpur. He was deeply learned in astrology. His wife was devout and saintly; she underwent hard penance for twelve years, worshipping the Ashwattha tree and the cow and praying that her progeny should survive. Her prayer was answered. Her only son, Bhaskarrao, who survived, entered the service of the Chief of the Sangli State, first as the head of a platoon in the army, and later as head clerk to the Chief. Later, the Sangli Chief appointed him Vakil to the East India Company's Government. He was known for his uprightness and candour. The Chief of Sangli, as a token of regard for him, granted him an estate. He was stout and healthy and lived in robust health up to the age of ninety-five. His eldest son, Amritrao Tatya, also tall and strong like his father, entered the service of the British and rose to be a Mamlatdar. He was a good horseman. He was well-versed in Sanskrit and the Shastras, and had written a commentary *on Purushasukta.* He also knew astrology. One of his four sons, Govindrao (father of Mahadeo Govind Ranade), also entered the service of the British. Later, on the recommendation of his superiors, he was given an important post in the service of Kolhapur State, where he held various high offices until he retired on pension.

As Ramabai Ranade records, "the men of the Ranade family were tall, brilliant, strong and valiant, industrious, and generous of heart."[1] Though they no longer followed the profession of priests, Hindu rituals, rigorous discipline enjoined by religion and familiarity with Hindu religious lore continued to be part of family tradition. Administrative service came to be assimilated into that tradition. In the service of the British, two generations of Ranades had humbly participated in the task of bringing order into revenue and judicial administration. This generated in their mind not only a preference for but also loyalty to the British rule. Govindrao, on one occasion, narrowly escaped imprisonment and humiliation at the hands of rebellious Sardars of Kolhapur because he was a British-appointed man; and only the timely arrival of British forces saved him from this calamity. The Ranades had entered the new class of society drawn from among Indians, which the British had created as the medium through which they contacted and governed the masses. This was the class through which beneficial as well as stern measures of the government were administered. Not all in this class were upright; but the Ranades were.

Mahadeo Govind Ranade was born on Tuesday, January 18, 1842, at Niphad in the Nasik district of Maharashtra. He was originally named 'Madhav', but somehow many persons began to call him 'Mahadeo', which he accepted. His father, Govindrao, was then head clerk to the Mamlatdar, earning a modest salary of about thirty-five rupees a month. In those days this amount was enough to provide bare comforts, and there was an expectation of promotion.

About two and a half years after this event, Govindrao, on the recommendation of his superior officer who was impressed by his efficiency, was appointed as Court Reader in the office of the Karbhari of Kolhapur State. This State had come under the control of the British only a few decades before. His wife, Gopikabai, was then in the family way. Govindrao, therefore, went to Kolhapur alone, leaving his wife and son with his mother at Niphad. The wife gave birth to a daughter who was named Durga. In due time, Gopikabai with her children went from Niphad to Ambegaon where Govindrao's father was staying, and then left Ambegaon for Kolhapur. Those were days before the railways were constructed. Journeys were made by bullock carts, and roads were rough. Gopikabai with the three year old Mahadeo and infant Durga, escorted by a peon accompanying the cart on foot, and a relation Vithu Kaka following on horseback, started the journey. The road was through fields and forests, hills and valleys. It was summer and travelling was done by night. The cart set out on one of the evenings, and the night was dark. After a time, the peon, tired of walking, mounted the cart and sat by the drivers side. Behind them was Gopikabai, with the infant hugged close to her bosom, and Mahadeo heavily wrapped in blankets, curled up between her and the edge of the cart. The cool breeze and the rattling of the cart gradually put to sleep everyone, including the driver, while the bullocks by themselves were pulling the cart onwards, through ups and downs. Suddenly there was a jolt, and the child Mahadeo slipped off from the cart. Amidst the rattling sound and overcome by fast sleep, none of the inmates of the cart noticed what had happened. Mahadeo lay where he fell, in the middle of the jungle, and in darkness, on the lonely road. He was unhurt, thanks to the thick woollen covering in which he was wrapped, but he was awake. He waited, quietly, without shouting or crying. About half an hour, later, when Vithu Kaka came along on the horseback, the boy called out, "Vithu Kaka. I have fallen here."[2] Vithu Kaka dismounted, picked up the boy and surprised the mother by presenting him to her.

This philosophic calmness was a trait unbecoming in a child of three. It made Ranade, as a boy, too silent; and the members of the family and friends thought that the silence signified lack of intelligence. Throughout his boyhood up to the age of fifteen, which Ranade spent at Kolhapur, he was considered a mediocre. Though he was healthy and well-built, he was by no means handsome. Taciturn, bashful and unimpressive, this only son was a great disappointment to his mother. "I wonder if Madhav will be able to earn even ten rupees a month and support his family,"[3] she used to say in despair. The impression was strengthened by a natural defect in his speech; he was unable to pronounce gutturals until the age of twelve. When he heard the result of an examination which he passed, he would not communicate the happy news to his family; when they heard it from others, they thought him to be abnormal and dull-witted on that account. When asked to explain why he did not speak of his success, he would say, "What is special about passing an examination successively with ease."[4]

Ranade, as a boy, was a stickler for details in his settled routine; once a procedure was fixed, he would follow it to the minutest detail, even if people ridiculed him. For some months, the routine was that on his coming home from school at 10 in the morning his mother would serve him with *chapatis*, pouring warm *ghee* on them from a particular vessel. One day, she served him with butter, and that too from another pot. Mahadeo refused, and could not at all be persuaded to take it. As there was no liquid *ghee* in the house, the mother put some water in the usual vessel, warmed it, and poured it on his chapati. That satisfied the boy. He had a craze for the habitual way!

He did not need to be chided or even reminded about the usual tasks expected from a boy of his age. His wife in her reminiscences quotes his aunt describing part of his day's routine: "After returning from school in the morning, he would have his breakfast, and thereafter as a rule, play a game of *sagargoti* (a game popular with girls) with Durga (his sister), and then go for a bath. With the first *lota* of water poured on his head, he would start reciting the *Purushasukta*,"[5] After the bath so accompanied by sacred words, he would follow the elaborate *sandhya* prayer. He could not stand being disturbed. Once he was interrupted by an elderly relation who put him a question pertaining to what he was reciting. He gave the correct answer, but lost the link. He was very much upset. "I will not begin from the beginning,"[6] he said. He would neither proceed, nor stop or get up; he compelled the interrupter to recite the whole *sandhya* up to the point where he was disturbed. The whole *sandhya* had to be said, and must be said. He wondered as to why should he suffer the penalty of repeating a long portion of it for others fault.

While at play, Ranade took defeat against other boys in a sporting spirit. Once, in the absence of companions, he had to play a game of dice with a wooden pillar imagined as the opponent. The dice for himself was played with one hand and for the pillar with the other. The pillar defeated him; but he did not mind this in the least. When teased by others about this defeat from even a pillar, he said, "The hand for the pillar got the deal. So it got the kill. I did not get the deal, so I was defeated. Where is disgrace in it?"[7]

Besides indoor games like dice and sagargoti, Mahadeo might also have played outdoor games of his time, but no account of them is available.

The boy had an inherent dislike for ostentation. On festive days, his mother coaxed him into wearing bracelets or a necklace. But he would hide the bracelets under his sleeve and cover the necklace with the end of the *dhoti*, and annoyance was evident on his face. On being asked, "Why must you hide the ornaments like a stupid fellow?"[8], he replied, "The *madhukaris* (the orphan or poor students whom the pious feed by rotation) have no ornaments!" Evidently he felt that ornaments made the wearer too conspicuous; at the same time he noted that poorer students, fundamentally not different, could get on well without this superfluity.

In those days children did not dare to speak with their father except when asked or permitted. Govindrao was never stern with his son, nor did he ever scold him; but the son kept himself at a distance, according to the custom of the day, and also because of inherent shyness. Mahadeo's closest companion in the house was his only sister, Durga, younger to him by two years and a half. Being the only son, his mother watched him every moment, anxious that he should grow, and worried about his apparent deficiencies. There was another lady in the house, Govindrao's brother's wife. Though the style of living was simple, there was no lack of comfort; for Govindrao's income was fairly good, and he was liberal in spending.

The Ranades lived on the ground floor of Government quarters. The first floor was occupied by the family of Kirtanes. Janardan Hari Kirtane was the Karbhari and Govindrao Ranade was Court Reader in his office. The two families developed great friendship; they lived like close relations, and celebrated most festivals together. Janardan Hari Kirtane's son Vinayak and Mahadeo became intimate friends. Imparting education to boys in a systematic way through a standardised type of schools was one of the many reforms introduced by the British. A few enlightened Indians, who were sent from British India to Kolhapur set up schools of the new type, a Marathi school in 1848 and an English school soon after. Mahadeo was put in these schools as and when they were started.

When he began attending the primary school he was quite fascinated by what he was learning. He used to mutter his lessons to himself and make letters and figures on walls with fingers. That was his recreation. Even when he was playing about in the street, he would sit down and write multiplication tables in the dust.

Mahadeo had completed his Marathi education by the time the English school was started. Nana Moroji, the enlightened gentleman who had taken the initiative in starting it, first ascertained from State officials as to who would be sending their sons to it, and Govindrao had given his consent. When the school started Mahadeo's name was on the roll. For three days, the boy did not go to school. The teacher reported the matter to Govindrao. The latter, on making enquiries, learnt that it was on the instruction of Gopikabai that the boy had not gone. She shared the general prejudice that English education alienated boys from their culture and their community, and led them to be converted to Christianity. This prejudice had some basis; the earlier English schools, which were started by the missionaries, did aim at proselytisation. Govindrao knew that English education by itself was not frightful, especially as the teachers and the managers of the school were his Hindu friends. He asked Mahadeo to attend the school in spite his mother's order, and the boy obeyed. On this, the mother became so despondent that she gave up food. Ultimately, after three days, the father succeeded in winning her over.

The school at Kolhapur, however, did not impart education beyond a limit, and further education could be had only at a place like Poona or Bombay. Gopikabai objected to the idea of sending Mahadeo out of the town, as she could not bear the separation of her only son, and Govindrao had to yield. However, Gopikabai soon died of child-birth. The affection which Govindrao had for his wife did not come in the way of his marrying again within sixteen days of her death as the force of customs was very strong those days. Soon after in 1854, Mahadeo, at the age of 13, was married to Sakhubai, daughter of Moropant Dandekar of Wai and sister of the wife of the ruling Chief of Ichalkaranji. Mahadeo's younger sister, was married about the same time, but a little earlier.

Janardan Hari Kirtane and Govindrao Ranade took a long time to decide about sending their sons away for further education. The reason for this delay of two years is not easy to guess. It is true that the distance between Kolhapur and Bombay was very long for the age of bullock carts, and that the boy's boarding and lodging arrangements had to be worked out with difficulty. Mahadeo, however, had no patience. As was the usual attitude of boys in those days, he held his father in awe, and was afraid of speaking to him; but he pestered his father's friend, Kirtane. Everyday he would get up early and stand near the door of Kirtane's room. When Kirtane got up and came out, he would say to him, "Abasaheb, when will you send us all to Bombay? Please speak to Bhausaheb and send us all to school in Bombay."[9] It is difficult to say whether his impatience was due to his being tired of sitting idle or to his yearning for a new environment; or it may be that he had heard the elders speak about the worthiness and prestige obtained by those who had received higher education. Ultimately, it was decided that the boys would be sent. About January 1857, Mahadeo and his friend Vinayak began their studies in Bombay in the Elphinstone Institution.

Ranade's official career may be said to have begun even while he was a student. On brilliantly passing the Matriculation examination, he was elected a Daxina Fellow, and as such was student as well as tutor during all his College career. As a fellow he taught a variety of subjects to junior classes: History, Geography, Mathematics, Economics, Logic and English Literature. On finishing his college career in 1866 he was appointed Marathi Translator in the Educational Department; and he had also to act as administrator of a small Indian State in Sholapur District. His subsequent appointments were: Judge in the State of Kolhapur (1867), Professor of English Literature in the Elphinstone College (1868-71), Police Magistrate at Bombay (1871), First Class Subordinate Judge at Poona (1871-78), Subordinate Judge at Nasik and Dhulia (1878-81), Subordinate Judge at Poona (1881), Special Sub-Judge under the Deccan Ryots' Relief Act (1881-84), Judge of the Small Cause Court at Poona (1884-85). Special Judge under the Relief Act (1885-93), Member of the Finance Committee of the Government of India (1886), and Judge of the Bombay High Court (1893-1901). In terms of emoluments, his salary which was Rs. 200 per month in 1866 as Marathi Translator, rose to Rs. 1,200 per month in 1884, and still higher when he became a High Court Judge.

A glance at this brief sketch of Ranade's official career shows that in the earlier period, Ranade had to perform an unusual variety of duties. Teacher and student of many subjects, Marathi Translator, reading and reviewing literature on all possible subjects, Administrator, Judge, Professor of Literature and Police Magistrate—these are the offices he held in the first ten years. In his acquaintance with several spheres and several aspects of society may be found the roots of his view that all departments of human life are inter-related, and that progress in one is not possible without progress in others.

Ranade entered public life while he was a student. The Association for the Spread of Knowledge (Dnyanprasarak Sabha), was the forum which he used in order to express his thoughts on subjects of social value. His interests in this period, 1859-64, are indicated by the subjects of his essays read before it, which were: 'Duties of Educated Indians', 'Maratha princes', 'Signs of future progress of Marathas and Bengalis—a comparative study,' 'Evil effects of overpopulation'. For some months in 1862-63, he edited the English section of a newly started paper, *Indu-prakash.*

Indu-prakash was a champion of social reform. Its sponsors represented a new sensitiveness to the misery and injustice of some of the centuries-old social customs among the Hindus. They started an association for the encouragement of widow-remarriages, of which Vishnushastri Pandit became the secretary; and Ranade joined it as a member. The orthodox Shastries started a counter-reform organisation. In 1869 the reformers arranged a widow-remarriage, and Ranade was one of the seven signatories to the invitation. Letters were sent to Vishnushastri Pandit threatening his life. The marriage was performed. The orthodox group organised a social boycott of all its supporters, and held meetings in various cities and towns of Maharashtra. Pandit challenged his opponents for a discussion, and one Shastri accepted it. In the meanwhile Ranade was writing letters to men of advanced views all over India to gather support to the cause. In 1870 the long awaited discussion was held at Poona, under the presidency of Shankaracharya, the ecclesiastical head of Maharashtra, with a panel of judges, selected by both sides. Ranade was one of the three who assisted Pandit. After nine days of debate the panel of judges gave their verdict against widow-remarriages. Shankaracharya announced *prayashchitta* or penance for the participants in the marriage. Ranade refused to do the penance, and chose to face excommunication. However, apart from occasional insults of his womenfolk and the difficulty in finding Brahmin servants, Ranade had not to suffer much, partly owing to his high official position and partly to the slowly widening support to the idea of widow-remarriage.[10] But this whole episode at the threshold of his public life must have had several effects on his general outlook and attitude. First, it must have hardened Ranade's resolve to remove the objectionable social customs; it explains the highest place Ranade gave to social reform in his public activities. Secondly, while searching for Shastric support for widow-remarriage, Ranade was introduced to the vast history of Hindu society as revealed in Sanskrit books; for, discrepancies in the injunctions of Shastras could partly be explained by the view that Hindu society was changing in the course of its long history. Thirdly, the authority of Shankaracharya over the Shastris and of the Shastris over the Hindu society might have led him to hold firmly that this situation was much similar to the hold of the Roman Catholic Church in medieval Europe. Fourthly, he might have thanked the British Government for preventing physical persecution of the reformers. And fifthly, this might have made him realise that social reform must at the same time be regarded as religious reform involving a change in religious views.

Besides the sponsors of Dnyanprakash, there was another group in Bombay which was equally zealous for social reform and which had already seen the necessity of bringing about religious reform as well. It included some of the old members of a defunct secret religious society named Paramahamsasabha and some young English-educated men of Ranade's age. This group held that efforts for social reform should more on spiritual than material good, which, after all, is the real purpose of life.[11] It started a new religious society named Prarthana Samaj in 1867. Ranade was attracted to this group and joined their society. Its creed was very much like that of Brahmo Samaj of Bengal; in fact the eloquent stirring speeches of the Brahmo Samaj leader Keshab Chandra Sen, during his visit in 1864 had encouraged this group to start this new society. The tenets which distinguished it from popular Hinduism of the day were the following: (1) God is one and without a form. (2) Image-worship is wrong and should be abandoned. (3) God should be worshipped through meditation and prayer and good actions. Injunctions implicit in this creed were abstaining from worshipping images at home or in temples, not observing caste distinctions, and removing the social customs which make lives of women unhappy, such as child-marriage, enforced celibacy of widows, etc. But subject to these broad principles, different members seemed to hold diverse views. Ranade undertook the task of systematizing these views and wrote in 1868 a comprehensive article entitled 'A Theist's Confession of Faith'. In it, Ranade states the position which logically followed the creed of Prarthana Samaj on the various problems of religion and metaphysics, such as the nature of religious knowledge, God, relation between God and man, soul and the problem of evil. Ranade, Bhandarkar and Modak were the foremost intellectuals in the Samaj.

In 1871 Ranade left Bombay and took up his post as Sub-Judge, at Poona. During his stay there for about seven years he galvanised the city of Poona with unprecedented energy and activity. He introduced in Poona the Western method of doing public work through institutions. The list of institutions which Ranade founded or which, being in existence before he arrived, were built by him is long and varied. It includes the following: The Sarvajanik Sabha (to discuss and to study public questions); the Poona N.G. Library; the Reay Museum; the Spinning and Weaving Company; the Metal Manufacturing Factory; the Fergusson College; the Female High School; the Arbitration Court (to settle disputes outside the law courts); the Poona Mercantile Bank; the Prarthana Samaj; the Oratory Encouragement Society; the Marathi Literature Encouragement Society; the Poona Spring Lecture Series; the Poona Dyeing Company; the Reay Paper Mill; and the Industrial

Association. The most notable among these was the Sarvajanik Sabha, started by the zealous patriot Ganesh Wasudeo Joshi. Ranade completely identified himself with this Sabha and very soon he and Joshi became its most respected leaders. "It became a pioneer for other provinces.... It aroused political consciousness and moulded political thought.... Under the influence of Ranade, the soul of Poona seemed to awake."[12]

Ranade's serious interest in Indian Economics dates from 1872, when he delivered a lecture on the foreign trade of India. The sudden increase of India's cotton trade with England with the commencement of the American Civil War in 1861, and its equally sudden breakdown with the cessation of the war in 1865, resulting first in the making and then in the un-making of many a fortune in India, may have directed his thoughts towards the nature of foreign trade. He deplored that India's imports consisted of manufactured goods; and pleaded that Indians must save and invest money in industries. He admired the people of France who, undaunted by the defeat of 1870, curtailed their expenses to the austerity level and built up their economy. Other studies in Indian Economics followed. His study of the Indian Revenue System in about 1874 was probably the basis of his view that the revenue was excessive; and the report of the Sarvajanik Sabha on the conditions of farmers in some districts in Bombay made him acutely conscious of the poverty and misery that stalked rural India. In 1876 a severe famine broke out in Poona, Nagar and Sholapur districts. The Sarvajanik Sabha organised the collection of complete information and the administration of relief. After the famine was over Ranade analysed its causes and showed that not failure of rain but the chronic poverty of the farmer was the true cause, and that the ultimate cause was the excessive land revenue imposed by the Government.

The death of Ranade's first wife in 1873 threw him into great grief. For the first time he was seen seeking consolation in religion. He recited to himself the devotional *Abhangas* of Tukaram, and on occasions burst into tears. He struggled with his grief to maintain hope and faith in God.[13]

There was, for the time being, a lull in the social reform activities. The social boycott against Ranade was gradually becoming ineffective. There were, however, two incidents. One was the storm of criticism against Ranade, from foes and friends alike, when he married his second wife. A staunch advocate of widow remarriage as he was, he should have married a widow; but he was also a believer in maintaining affection among members of the family, and had a tender regard for the feelings of his strictly orthodox father. The other episode was the humiliation which he and his co-workers had to suffer when they participated in the procession of Swami Dayanand in 1875; the orthodox party in Poona literally threw mud on them.

It may be said that Ranade began to take part in politics in 1874. This he did through articles and memoranda which did not bear his name. Poona Sarvajanik Sabha served him as a blind. In 1874 the Sabha sent a petition to the British Parliament, requesting that the Parliament should include among its members, a few representatives of India, and that questions relating to Indian administration should be decided in consultation with them. In 1875 he caused the Sabha to send a memorial to the Viceroy urging that every chance should be given to Malharrao Gaekwad of Baroda to secure justice in his criminal trial, and that the State should not be abolished whatever be the verdict on the conduct of the ruler. A little later, there were riots in Nagar and Sholapur districts, in which the money-lenders were the targets of mob violence. Ranade made a penetrating analysis of the riots. He argued that the ultimate responsibility for them lay with the Government who, by levying excessively high land revenue, did not leave any choice to the cultivator but to borrow from the hard-hearted money-lender. The Government was enraged at these activities of the Sabha; and after another memorial of the Sabha proving that the Government were responsible for the famine of 1877, it was exasperated. It knew that Ranade controlled and guided the Sabha, and transferred him from Poona to Nasik.

During the three years that Ranade was away from Poona, he continued to criticise the administration. He got the Poona Sarvajanik Sabha to hold a public meeting to protest against the passing of the Press Act. He drafted in persuasive language the petition which the Sabha sent to the Viceroy on this subject. The Government wrongly suspected him of complicity with rebellion of Vasudeo Balwant Phadke in 1879 and transferred him to Dhulia, a place still smaller and still further away from Poona. Ranade wrote in the *Sarvajanik Sabha Journal* that, except in that case of Vasudeo Balwant, the motive of the rioters was economic, and not political as believed by officials. Scanning the evidence like a trained judge that he was, he once again proved that it was poverty of the people which caused the riots, and that the revenue policy of the Government aggravated the poverty.

In persisting in criticising the British administration, Ranade was only representing the prevailing temper among Indians. The policy followed by Lord Lytton since his arrival in India had antagonised the people; and to suppress the discontent he passed two acts of repression, the *Vernacular Press Act* and the *Indian Arms Act* of 1878. These developments probably made Ranade revise his attitude of admiration towards the British rule. It was probably as a result of this reconsideration that he developed the idea that there were two sharply distinct sections in the British nation, *Conservatives* and *Liberals*, and that the virtues attributed to the British nation were the virtues of the Liberals only. Following his lead, the Sarvajanik Sabha issued an appeal to the British electorate to vote for the Liberal Party.

A report of one of his lectures shows that as late as in 1878, Ranade had a low opinion of Indian learning. He criticised the view that Indians too have a rich heritage of literature and sciences. Indian learning, according to him, at its very best was but at the infant stage, altogether inferior to the Western. At the very same time, he had developed a very great respect for Hindu Philosophy. Writing in 1878 on the views of Dadoba Pandurang, a pioneer of religious reform in Bombay, he says, "It is a great relief to find that as a result of fifty years' study, Dadoba, though he reveres the holy Bible, ... has failed to accept the current doctrines of the Christian religion as a satisfactory solution of the problems of life and death ... Dadoba has more affinities and points of agreement with the philosophy and mysticism of the old Hindu religion..."[14] Then he proceeds to show these affinities, and also how old Hindu Philosophy is superior to the current Christian doctrines.

Ranade's mind continued to be largely occupied with administrative and political questions between 1881 and 1886. The harsh regime of the Conservative Lord Lytton was followed by the sympathetic regime of the Liberal Lord Ripon. This seemed to accord with Ranade's theory that the British rule could continue to be beneficent provided the Liberals held power in England. Ripon's Scheme of Local Self-Government had thrilled the educated Indians who had only read of democracy in books; and Ranade expounded to them the theory about the functions of a representative. The Ilbert Bill controversy in 1883-84 showed the helplessness of the Liberal Viceroy against European officials; and when the controversy ended, Ranade wrote an article in which he drew some conclusions. One was that the educated Indians represented the soul of Indian liberalism. Another, that the bureaucracy in India were supported by vested interests and were a conservative force determined to maintain the power and privilege of few. And while recognising the necessity of the protection given to India by the British rule, he said, "But it is not as the representative of brute force, but of the order and genius of equal law, that we bow down to this Supreme necessity."[15] This controversy was one of the contributory factors to the rise of nationalism and the founding of the Indian National Congress in 1885. Ranade was one of its founders.

After 1885 Ranade's interests seemed to have shifted away from politics. In the next few years he focused on religion, especially Hindu religion, and social reform. In 1885 he passionately defended religion, *Dharma-bhavana,* against the agnostic attack of Agarkar, and stated, "We Hindus love Dharma more than our lives; and whatever be the value of the opinions of Mill and Spencer to England, for India they are of no use".[16] There is, in this remark, a suggestion that a field in which Hindu culture is superior is of much importance. Again, in the same year, he pleaded for religious education in schools. He engaged himself in culling out from the Hindu religious books, statements on women's rights, and wrote an essay on the subject. In 1886 he delivered a lecture in Madras on 'Hindu Ideals of Duty' and proved that in respect of ideals, in no other society is there so much consciousness of duties as among the Hindus. In 1887, he said, "The religion of Hindus, unlike that of the Christians does not ask them to pray for bread; our religion tells us that we are sent by God in this world, not for enjoyment of pleasures of this world but to prepare for a life beyond."[17] Ranade suggested, with more emphasis than before, that superiority of the Hindu religion amounts to superiority of Indians in a very important field. Ranade prepared an essay on 'The *Sutra* and *Smriti* Dicta on Hindu Marriage' to prove Shastric support to adult marriages.

The social reform movement which had abated between 1870 and 1885 again acquired force. A letter written by Ranade to a new enthusiast, Malabari, provoked a controversy. In that letter, Ranade had approved of the principle that legislation was a legitimate method of bringing about social reform. This principle was hotly debated, especially with reference to its application to the Age of Consent; and the two camps were engaged in a fierce controversy for over a decade. Unlike the one of the earlier years, in this controversy many English-educated men also were seen in the camp opposed to the social reformers. Prominent among them was Bal Gangadhar Tilak. It is needless to recount the various incidents in this strife. But the question as to why English educated men, to whom social evils should be obvious, opposed reform deserves some explanation. A new feeling was emerging in the country by about 1880, a feeling of admiration for things Indian, and of contempt for things British. This created a tendency to minimise the evil nature of Indian social customs and to resent any interference with them by a foreign government. In spite o this accession of a new force to the opposition, Ranade founded the Indian Social-Conference in 1887, the meetings of which were held in the pandal of the Indian National Congress; and Ranade's annual addresses to it are valuable for clarity as well as profundity of thought on questions of social reform.

It is difficult to say whether the rise of this new, passionate, exclusive type of nationalism had any connection with the decline in the number of political utterances of Ranade after 1891. This exclusive nationalism did run counter to the older one on several points. The differences were stressed in Maharashtra more than in any other province. Feelings between the two groups were embittered. The band of national workers which clustered round

Ranade was virulently attacked by the new nationalists, whose very progressiveness in politics made them indifferent to social reform and antagonistic to its promotion by state legislation.

In 1892, Ranade delivered his famous lecture on 'Indian Political Economy' which gave a clear exposition of his new point of view in the study of economic problems of India. He showed that the conclusions of the classical economics of Adam Smith and Ricardo were not applicable to Indian conditions and that the policy of *laissez faire* pursued by the Government of India was injurious to the country. He pleaded that the Government should take bold measures for directly promoting industry and agriculture.

The conflict between the social reformers and the non-reformers in Maharashtra came to a head in 1895. The Social Conference used to be held in the *pandal* of the Indian National Congress. Opponents of social reform had been objecting to this practice since 1889; but their voice was negligible. In 1895, the Congress was to be held in Poona, which was the stronghold of the orthodox group. Tilak supported their view. Three or four of the social reformers were beaten; one member of the orthodox group threatened to set fire to the pandal. A false rumour was set afloat that the majority of Provincial Congress Committees were opposed to the use of the *pandal* by the Social Conference. The storm subsided only when, in the end, Ranade declared that the Social Conference would be held elsewhere. How deep was the agony he felt, and how nobly he endured the persecution to which he was subjected is revealed in the following passage from the lecture he delivered in the Social Conference of that year: "We have all to learn what it is to bear and forbear—to bear ridicule, insults, even personal injuries at times and forbear from returning abuse for abuse. In the words of the Prophet of Nazareth, we have to take up the cross, not because it is pleasant to be persecuted, but because the pain and the injury are as nothing by the side of the principle for which they are endured."[18]

In 1896 Ranade founded the Deccan Sabha in Poona, an organisation of his own followers who were stifled and practically ousted from the Sarvajanik Sabha by the new nationalists. But about this time his health began to deteriorate. Yet he never spared himself, and worked as hard as ever. In addition to his onerous duties as Judge of the High Court, he continued to attend the numerous meetings, lectures and conferences. Historical research and University reform were new fields he added to his sphere of work. In 1898-99 he was studying the problems before the Famine Commission and scanning the Peshwa's Diaries.

In November 1900 he unveiled the portrait of Dadabhai Naoroji, in Framji Cowasji Institute. That was his last public speech. His heart disease developed rapidly; and on the 16th January 1901 he passed away.

REFERENCES

1. Ranade, Ramabai, *Amchya Ayushatil Kahil Athavani* (trnsl.) by Kusumavati Deshpande, Ranade, His Wife's Reminiscences (New Delhi: Publications Division, Ministry of Information and Broadcasting), 1963, p. 17.
2. Jagirdar, P. J., *Mahadeo Govind Ranade* (New Delhi: Publications Division, Ministry of Information and Broadcasting, Government of India), 1971, p. 5.
3. *Ibid.*
4. *Ibid.*
5. Ranade, Ramabai, *Amchya Ayushatil Kahil Athavani* (trnsl.) by Kusumavati Deshpande, Ranade His Wife's Reminiscences, op. cit., p. 22.
6. *Ibid.*
7. Jagirdar, P. J., *Mahadeo Govind Ranade, op. cit.*, p. 7.
8. *Ibid.*
9. *Ibid.*, p. 9.
10. Jagirdar, P. J., *Studies in the Social Thought of M.G. Ranade* (New York: Asia Publishing House), 1963, p. 7.
11. *Ibid.*
12. Kellock, James, *Mahadev Govind Ranade, Patriot and Social Servant* (New Delhi: Rupa & Co.), 2003, p. 68.
13. Jagirdar, P. J., *Studies in the Social Thought of M.G. Ranade, op. cit.*, p. 9.
14. Ranade, Ramabai, *Miscellaneous Writings of the Late Hon'ble Mr. Justice M. G. Ranade* (New Delhi: Sahitya Akademi), 1992, pp. 57-58.
15. *Ibid.*
16. Jagirdar, P. J., *Studies in the Social Thought of M.G. Ranade, op. cit.*, p. 12.
17. *Ibid.*
18. Ranade, Ramabai, *Miscellaneous Writings of the Late Hon'ble Mr. Justice M.G. Ranade* (New Delhi: Sahitya Akademi), 1992.

2

IDEOLOGY AND PERCEPTION

The period covered by Ranade's life almost exactly synchronises with what is known as the Victorian Age. So far as India is concerned, the two main political features of India were, first, the consolidation of the British Empire and, secondly, a change in attitude of the Indian people towards the Empire, from contentment to discontent.

In the history of the British in India, the century between 1748 and 1848 was a period of conflict, conquest and expansion. There was Anglo-French conflict in 1748-60, Anglo-Muslim conflict in 1757-1801, Anglo-Maratha conflict in 1774-1818, and Anglo-Sikh conflict in 1845-49, in all of which the British emerged victorious. The British were superior in their military strength, organising power, methods of administration, art of diplomacy, political energy, scientific equipment and patriotic sentiment.

Consolidation was already begun in the period of conflict and conquest. Lord William Bentinck's regime from 1828 to 1835 is noted for the abolition of the *Suttee* and the suppression of *Thuggee.* In 1835, the Government embarked on a policy of promoting education in European literature and Sciences. Lord Dalhousie created a separate Public Works Department and started the making of roads, the building of irrigation canals, and the construction of railways; he also introduced the telegraphs. But consolidation acquired speed after the Great Rebellion of 1857 was suppressed and the Government of India was transferred from the East India Company to the British Crown in 1858. There were many aspects of this work of consolidation—law-making, improved organisation of the judiciary, administrative organisation, organisation of legislature and repression of forces opposed to the British rule.

Great codes of law were promulgated: the Code of Civil Procedure in 1859, the Indian Penal Code in 1860, and the Code of Criminal Procedure in 1861. A massive judicial machinery, divided and graded according to the type and seriousness of the dispute, with appeals to higher courts and ultimately to the Privy Council, was erected. Land Revenue administration was thoroughly organised, as also other branches of administration. Law and order were firmly established. Large irrigation schemes were carried out. A system of roads was constructed by which vast areas were connected and development of commerce was helped. Railways, telegraphs and cheap postal communication, apart from helping trade, added unexpected and hitherto unknown comforts to the life of the common man. Schools, colleges and universities imparting education of the Western type were established to impart education at all levels to continually increasing number of youths. These achievements of the British rulers brought about a change of such immensity in the national life that it would be no exaggeration to call it a revolution.

The constitutional developments of this period were another aspect of this consolidation. It was thought that the chief among the causes of the Indian Revolt of 1857 was the lack of any touch between the ruler and the ruled. It was felt that the addition of Indian element to the legislative councils would bring about this contact. The principle of associating Indians with the government of their own country was gradually and cautiously adopted. The Indian Councils Act of 1861 enlarged the Executive Council of the Governor-General by the addition of the fifth member who had to be a jurist, and, for the purpose of making laws, by the addition of six to twelve members, the majority of whom should be non-officials. It also restored to the Governments of Madras and Bombay where similar councils were established, powers of making laws. Among those nominated to the Indian Council in 1862 were three Indians.[1] The Indian Councils Acts of 1870 and 1892 increased the number of additional members and enabled the Governor-General to nominate members who had been elected. Further, they gave the councils power to discuss—though not to vote—the budget and to ask questions.

The consolidation of the British Empire in India also required some measures to curb down such opposition as might arise. Perhaps the most important of these measures were the new army policy after the Revolt of 1857, and the Indian Arms Act. Lack of confidence in Indian men and officers, and a desire to keep Indians divided among themselves, were the motives behind this new army policy. The army in India was reorganised on the basis of three principles: (i) Retaining in the country an irresistable force of British troops; (ii) Keeping artillery in the hands of Europeans, and (iii) Preserving distinctiveness among different groups within which differences and rivalries are most marked. Consequently, among other steps taken, one was that the regiments drew recruits from three or four different races and recruiting grounds, but the men of each class or race were kept apart in separate companies. The Indian Arms Act of 1878 made it a criminal offence to keep, bear or traffic in arms without licence. Heavy penalties were prescribed to enforce provisions of the Act; and by rules made under the Act, Europeans were exempted from its jurisdiction.

The second political feature of this period, namely, a change of attitude of the Indian people towards the Empire from contentment to discontent, arises from these governmental policies and constitutional development. Whatever may have been the obstacles the British had to encounter in the course of their expansion, hatred for foreigners was not among them. On the contrary, there is evidence to show that some powerful elements in the country actually supported them. Shejwalkar in the quarterly journal of *Bharat-Itihasa-Samshodak-Mandal* (Year 6th, Number 1) in a paper entitled 'Indian Helpers of the Founders of the British Rule', shows that one family of the commercial class named 'Gupta' was of enormous help to the spread of British dominion in India.[2] From the time of Clive in 1765 to that of Canning in 1858 this family not only gave financial help to the British but secured useful military information about the Indian rulers' territories for the British. Javadekar, in his *Adhunik Bharat,* argues on the basis of this instance that the whole commercial class supported the British conquest of India. He also quotes P. E. Roberts, who says, "The revolution in Bengal in 1756-57 was, in the main, not the conquest of an Indian province by a European colonial power; its true nature was that indigenous commercial and money-lending classes, collaborating with the British overthrew a foreign (Muslim) rule."[3] While this view cannot be accepted without further evidence, and the whole merchant class may not have actually participated in the extension of the British dominion, it is certain that this class could not have in the least regretted the disappearance of utterly selfish, feeble and warring local Indian rulers and must have welcomed the firm rule of the British. Moreover, in Bengal the rule overthrown by the British was that of Muslim chiefs whereas the merchant class was that of the Hindus, and to the latter the change of government was that of one foreign government for another.[4] It is true that in Maharashtra the rulers were Hindus and it is possible that the commercial class was not so large or influential; but on the other hand, not only was the rule of the last Peshwas incompetent and unpopular but, if the evidence of *Lokahitawadi* is to be relied on, several Sardars in the Deccan, lured by the promises of the British and foolishly hoping to receive pensions without having to render any service, had gone over voluntarily to the side of the British. The common man also had not the slightest reason to prefer the chaotic rule of the Indian rulers to the orderly rule of the British Company. The merchant class and the common people were, then, either happy or indifferent at the transfer of power to the British. Thus the British conquest in India began with the goodwill of several classes in India.

Conscious that resentment against any foreign rule is natural, the British Government in India had followed certain principles to mitigate it. In the first place, they refrained from wounding the religious susceptibilities of the communities of India. Secondly, they spread Western learning; and though they thought that after a few centuries this would inevitably impel Indians to demand elimination of the British rule, they held that for some centuries the English-educated class would be a great support to the British rule. Thirdly, Elphinstone and Malcolm had adopted the policy of pleasing those Indian rulers and *jagirdars* who had accepted the British rule, so that these also could be depended on. Fourthly, they gave a certain amount of liberty for advocating religious and social reform. Metcalf held the opinion that liberty of the press, for many years, would be used not for attaining political freedom but for religious and social reform; and this forecast proved to be correct. Thus the British had deliberately created their supporters; and these stood by them in the Great Rebellion of 1857. In their petition in 1857 to continue to maintain their political rule, the East India Company says, "That our policy has been successful has been proved by the following things: At the time of the Mutiny, which is supposed to have been caused by the fear of danger to religion, Indian rulers and Indian people remained loyal to the British Government. Had Indian rulers, instead of helping to curb the Mutiny, assumed its leadership, or had common people joined it, the result of the recent happenings would have been totally different." It is not true that the common people did not join the 'mutiny'. Though, too late, the realisation had dawned on the country that the British coming from 5,000 miles away were foreigners in a sense in which Indian Muslims were not. But the forces of appreciation and contentment were strong enough to nullify, to a large extent, forces of discontent. In Maharashtra, they were decidedly stronger.

After 1870, however, discontent began to increase. Several factors contributed to this result. Prominent among them was the economic factor. India was being impoverished by the destruction of her industries which could not stand the competition of foreign, machine made goods; the unemployed artisans having taken to agriculture, the pressure on land inceased; and in years of monsoon failure poverty of farmers led to several famines. Taxation of land was heavy. The second factor was the increase of racial bitterness between the rulers and the ruled. The Revolt of 1857 created utter distrust of Indians in the hearts of Englishmen. The Arms Act of 1878 disarmed all Indians. The Ilbert Bill controversy further embittered racial feelings (Under the then existing laws, Europeans outside the Presidency towns could be tried by European judges and not by any Indian judge. The Government, to remove this discrimination, introduced a bill known as the Ilbert Bill in 1883. The Europeans stiffly resisted this just measure and carried on strong agitation. The Act which was ultimately passed by way of a compromise was a triumph of the European view). The influence of the press was another factor. Although for some years after the introduction of printing in India, the press was engaged in the criticism of Indian society, a time came when it turned its critical attention to the actions of the Government. The influence of English literature contributed to the growth of discontent in a peculiar manner. Western education instilled in the minds of Indians the concepts of freedom, nationalism, and democracy. It was but natural that they should strive to realise these grand conceptions in their own country. Foreign rule was the denial of all these conceptions.

Thus, on the one hand, the resentment against the unjust and callous deeds of the British Government and the British people, and on the other hand, the rise of patriotic sentiment, created feelings of discontent. In the meanwhile, the novelty of the beneficent measures of the British Government was worn out. It can be said that towards the end of the nineteenth century the feeling of discontent against the British rule was distinctly greater than that of contentment.

So great was this discontent that according to one version, the Indian National Congress was founded in 1885 in order to allay it. The discontent was aggravated after the famine of 1877. "Mr. Hume—the Father of the Congress—had seen government reports... which disclosed that the masses were seething with discontent and were becoming desperate. It was likely that some bitter young men from among the educated classes would take the lead, organise the people, and direct it as a national revolt."[5]

This actually happened in one instance. In Maharashtra, in 1879, Wasudeo Balwant Phadke had led such a rebellion from real patriotic motives. Neither suppression of this or such rebel nor opening channels; of constitutional criticism through the Indian National Congress, could have eliminated the national discontent.

Economic life in India was entirely transformed during the course of the nineteenth century. Three chief features of this transformation were: (i) competition of foreign manufactures, (ii) changes in the character and vicissitudes in the fortunes of Indian agriculture, and (iii) tardy growth of modern manufactures in India.

Though commerce between India and the West had been going on for centuries, it had not affected the economic structure in India till the nineteenth century. It was only when there was a series of new inventions, which brought about the industrial revolution that the English manufacturer gained great superiority over the Indian artisan, and that as a consequence trade with the West, affected the economic structure of India. Even in the nineteenth century, the effects were felt only after 1850 or 1860, with the opening up of India by means of roads, railways and the new steamship routes. The old economic structure, with its predominantly agricultural and rural population, with its towns, the industries of which depended on their being centres of pilgrimage or court life, with its villages economically self-sufficient and each having a majority of artisans as the servants of the village, began to be transformed. The handicrafts of Indian urban industries had attained a high degree of excellence and their reputation was world-wide; but the disappearance of native Indian Courts and competition of foreign machine-made goods gave them a great blow. "India in the eighties afforded the spectacle of a huge country which decaying handicrafts, with any other form of organised industry almost non-existent and a consequent falling back upon land."[6]

The British administration of India created new problems for Indian agriculture, which even before was not in a very prosperous condition. Apart from depriving cultivators of ownership in areas where Zamindari was created, the new judicial system put the cultivator in a disadvantageous position *vis-a-vis* the money-lender. In pre-British days, the existence of a vigorous village community and the practice of the state leaving disputes to be settled by village Panchayats were two restraints on the money-lender. Under the British rule these checks were largely removed. After 1850, the Indian farmer was brought into contact with the world market, and as about the same time the discovery of gold mines in Australia and California and of silver mines in California increased the supply of precious metals, a large quantity of these metals found their way into India, and there was a general tendency towards increase of prices. During the American Civil War in the sixties, the British Textile Industry placed orders for cotton in India, and the consequent rise in its price was a source of profit to cultivators of all the cotton-growing tracts. The decade 1860-70 was a period of prosperity for the cultivators. But the very prosperity gave greater opportunity for borrowing; and when the slump came, the position of the cultivator suddenly became bad. The British had given rights of free transfer and absolute ownership to the cultivators, which they had never possessed before, and thus, the temptation as well as opportunities to borrow increased. There began a movement of a gradual transference of land, from the hands of the original cultivators to the money-lenders. This created agrarian discontent which led to murderous uprisings of peasants, such as the Santhal rebellion (1855), the Deccan riots (1874), and the riots of Ajmer (1891). To add to the difficulties of the problem, there was a series of famines in the decade 1870-80. In the next decade, as there were no famines, a new tendency began to appear—a tendency of the export of wheat and raw produce. This was a further effect of India being drawn into the world market by the developments in communications.

New forms of industry were introduced into India. These were plantations and factories. From the beginning, the plantations were European-owned, and they grew enormously during 1860-70. Wherever these were established, as in Bengal, the condition of peasants became far worse. The factory industry also developed after 1854 but its growth was extremely slow. "While the process of driving out people from their old crafts was proceeding quickly, the growth of new industries to absorb the people thus displaced was in no sense proportionate."[7] In the matter of decay or growth of industries, the British Government of India strictly adhered to the principle of *laissez faire*, and refrained from leading a helping hand. On the contrary, it sometimes went out of its way to give direct assistance to English manufacturers in exploiting the Indian market. This was evident in its railway policy and the tariff policy during the nineteenth century.

The transformation of Indian Society in the nineteenth century which resulted from the contact of the West is one of the greatest movements of the age. For, on the one hand, it covered a people numbering several hundreds of millions; and, on the other, it resulted in far-reaching changes over a very wide field of social life.

There is a similarity between the effect of the West on India's economic life and that on her cultural life. India's cultural contact with the West is centuries old; but it had not affected India's life till the nineteenth century. It was only when there was a rapid growth of scientific knowledge, resulting from the newly developed freedom of reason, that the English learning gained a superiority over the decaying Hindu and Muslim learning in India. Even in the nineteenth century, the effects were felt only after 1850 or 1860, when, fifteen or twenty-five years following the Government's adoption of the policy of encouraging Western knowledge, there was quite a good number of Indians who had acquired that knowledge, had developed enthusiasm for it, and had come to occupy a good status in the new set-up of Indian society under the British rule. The notions about material universe prevailing in India could not withstand the challenge of truths discovered by scientific methods in the West. New truths of physics, chemistry, astronomy and biology threw new light on metaphysical, ethical and social problems, and thoughtful Indians had to modify the structure of traditional knowledge, beliefs and social customs in this new light.

Two currents of Western culture were being poured into India, the Christian religion, and scientific knowledge. Indeed, under the East India Company and also under the Crown of the British, Government of India had adopted the policy of not interfering with indigenous religions; nevertheless the rulers believed that Indians could not rise either materially or spiritually unless they ultimately adopted Christianity. The missionaries were enthusiastic, and missed no opportunity of running down the beliefs, the tenets and the injunctions of the Hindu religion in social matters. However, the Christian religion itself was having quarrel with the new science in the West. During the seventeenth, eighteenth and nineteenth centuries, reason had been steadily destroying Christian mythology and exposing the pretensions of supernatural revelation. In the nineteenth century, the discoveries of science in many fields, first in geology, then in zoology, and afterwards in anthropology bore with full force upon the fabric of Christianity, and historical criticism of scriptures methodically undermined their authority.[8] The most intense literary attack on orthodox Christianity was from 1870-82. This controversy had its effect on the several stages of cultural transformation in India during the century.

Cultural and social life in India, on which the Western culture made its impact, was at a low level and deteriorating due to chaotic political conditions. Social institutions were largely controlled by religion, and, generally speaking, the religion of India was Hinduism. "Seven Hundred years of Islamic authority over (the country)... had left Hinduism in a state of depression. It was the religion of a subject race, looked down on with contempt by the Muslims as idolatry. It enjoyed no prestige and for many centuries its practice had been tolerated only under considerable disadvantage in various areas. It had no central direction, no organisation and hardly any leadership."[9] In the absence of leadership and state-guidance, there grew up in Hindu society a number of socially harmful customs, widely varying among different sections of the community. In the field of religion, Hinduism permitted of several and often contradictory faiths and beliefs. The state of education also was unsatisfactory. The schools which kings, Hindus and Muslims, had founded flourished owing to their munificence; but war and strife made this munificence impossible. "Profound and universal ignorance was the natural consequence."[10] Indian learning, though much more advanced than the Western in ancient times, had remained at a standstill for several centuries past and was being neglected and forgotten; and owing to the barrier of the language, it remained cut off from the whole development of learning and science which took place in Europe from the seventeenth century onwards.

The spread of English language in India removed an age-long barrier between the cultures at a time when there was great disparity between them; and establishment of law and order made growth, of learning again possible. Far-reaching changes in the cultural and social life in India were inevitable. The West had also confronted other Asiatic countries like China and Japan in a similar way. Panikkar, in his *Asia and Western Dominance,* regards the social revolution in India as part of the renaissance of Asia. In his brilliant analysis of this renaissance, he points out its four broad characteristics; and on closer consideration these are found to be the most salient features of Indian revolution.[11]

In the first place, the reorganisation of society was the work of thinking men at the top, not the result of the awakened conscience of the masses. Only few could have learnt the foreign, English language; and of them, only a small minority could have conquered the innate tendency of conservatism. Reform movement was never a mass movement in the nineteenth century, except in Arya Samaj where it was linked up with vigorous opposition to foreign cultures. Even Arya Samaj had to face the opposition of the majority which was partly due to its programme of social reform. Except Swami Dayanand, all other reformers were English-knowing and appreciative of English learning, including Ram Mohun Roy, Balashastri Jambhekar, Lokahitvadi, the members of the Paramahamsa Mandali, Jyotiba Phule, Ranade, Vishnupant Pandit, Swami Vivekananda, and the founders of the Theosophical Society. The conservative minority not only kept aloof but was intolerant, and persecution of religious and social reformers through social boycott and slander was usually to be expected. It is this fear of persecution which explains why the Paramahamsa Mandali, a society of believers in religious and social reform founded in Bombay in 1840, was a secret organisation and why it broke down immediately after the names of its members were made known to the public. Balashastri Jambhekar who readmitted a man from Christianity to Hinduism had to suffer social boycott for five years; and Jyotiba Phule's wife had to suffer the insult of being hit with stones because she was a teacher in a school for girls started by her husband. The persecution, however, was held in check by two factors: first that intolerance had not developed as a tradition as it had in medieval Europe, and second, that the foreign British Government protected reformers against criminal attacks.

In the second place, efforts at social reform always involved religious reform. Without religious reform, social reform was not possible. This was so for two reasons: Firstly, the hold of religion on the minds of Indians was strong, and it was not loosened by attacks of Reason as it was in the West; so that it was easier to change society through a change in religion sanctioning the social change. Secondly, as Swami Vivekananda pointed out with regard to the caste system, all social institutions were wrongly held to be religious institutions; so that social and religious reforms were identical. Thus Ram Mohun Roy (1772-1833) founded the Brahmo Samaj which joined ideas of social reform, like raising the status of women, fighting the caste-system, condemning polygamy and other social abuses to the system of philosophy of the Vedanta. Balashastri Jambhekar (1810-46), who induced a friend to write a book on widow remarriage, was also a religious reformer inasmuch as he stood for reconversion of man originally a Hindu from Christianity. The chief tenets of Paramahamsa Mandali included principles of social reform like ignoring caste differences and supporting widow marriages as well as religious principles like abstaining from worshipping idols. Jyotiba Phule (1828-90) who started a girls' school in 1848, a school for untouchables in 1854, and an orphanage to prevent infanticide in 1863, founded also a religious organisation named 'Satya-Shodhak Samaj' to preach (i) oneness of God who is all-pervading, (ii) right of all men to worship God without the mediation of priests, and (iii) abolition of distinctions based on birth. Ranade founded the Prarthana Samaj.[12] The Arya Samaj and the Theosophical Society were primarily religious reform organisations which included social reform as an essential part of their programmes.

The third feature of the transformation of India was the attempt to assimilate the learning and thought of the West. With the exception of Swami Dayanand, every reformer set a high value on Western learning. As stated earlier, Western culture included two currents—Christianity and modern science. Both these parts of Western culture were opposed to each other, and some thinkers, such as leaders of the Broad Church movement, were attempting a reconciliation between the two. By and large, India was un-impressed by Christianity. Except the oppressed classes in Hindu society, all Hindus sharply resented attempts to propagate or spread Christianity. But all reformers made it more or less their mission to acquire and spread the new Western knowledge. Ram Mohun Roy was one of the pioneers of Western education in India and an ardent advocate of a combination of Eastern and Western knowledge in the educational system; he established 'The Hindu College of the Western type in Calcutta in 1817. Balashastri Jambhekar was apparently overjoyed to see the wealth of the Western knowledge and greedily collected all he could. He studied nine languages, wrote articles and books on numerous subjects including history, mathematics, psychology and grammar, started the first weekly journal in Maharashtra, and tried to establish a library and a debating society. Ranade, the Prince among graduates, was one amongst the men who were most learned in Western knowledge. Even Tilak and Chiplunkar who dreamt of the cultural glory of ancient India established a school, which developed into a college of the Western type; and the followers of Swami Dayanand spread a network of D.A.V. Colleges in North-Western India. Western learning has become part and parcel of the cultural heritage of modern India.

The fourth characteristic of the cultural transformation of India was the gradual growth of nationalism. "The growth of national feeling was the direct result of the reaction against Western aggression," says Panikkar.[13] Yet this reaction was slow to develop, because of the peculiar circumstances and the character of the British conquest of India. As written above, in the earlier half of the nineteenth century, there was more contentment than discontent, and to enlightened minds contact with the Westerners even as rulers seemed to offer the only hope of the progress of people. But sooner or later, resentment against foreign rule was inevitable, and, as a result of forces already indicated above, the last quarter of the nineteenth century saw a rapid growth of national feeling in India.

Opinions seem to differ as to the nature of the whole social transformation as it has turned out to be. One writer, Humayun Kabir, describes it by saying, "The old was destroyed beyond recall but the new remains still unborn".[14] According to him, only a free India would have attempted a synthesis. According to Marvin, towards the end of the nineteenth century renascence of the ancient books and thought of India took place, though the question still arose and remained undecided as to whether the ideal was to be a reversion to a golden age of the past or a pressing forward to a new age of a modern Western type. Panikkar describes it as a synthesis between the East and the West. And a fourth writer, Zinkin, describes the transformation as Westernisation. In his *Asia and the West,* he says, "Behind the Westernisation of India's institutions lay a far more significant fact, the Westernisation of its mind." Which of these views is correct? Is India's transformation, resulting from the contact with the West, a mere destruction of the old without any new construction, or is it a renascence of old teaming and thought, or is it a synthesis of the East and the West, or is it, at least in its final outcome, Westernisation?

"Indian in blood and colour, but English in taste, in opinions, in morals and in intellect", such was Macaulay's conception of the type to be produced by the educational policy he proposed. Study of the thought of Mahadeo Govind Ranade reveals the measure of success this policy achieved in the first generation produced by it. Born in a Brahmin family, Ranade was brought up strictly as a Hindu. But his mind drew its nourishment entirely from Western learning during the period of his education. It was with marvellous avidity that he, while a student, read everything available on all subjects in humanities.

On the whole, it would be proper to regard Ranade as a thinker in the English tradition, but greatly concerned with renovating Indian society and seeking points of affinity with the Indian tradition of thought. It could be said that he was alien in outlook and Indian in sympathies, alien in mind and Indian at heart. He left his home in Kolhapur to study in Bombay at the age of twelve; thus, in the formative period of his life he was not only subjected to the influence of English learning but was somewhat removed from the cultural influences of the home. His studious habits made him spend more time with English authors than with his Indian fellow students. He frankly said in 1861, "I know very little of Brahmanical Schools— either their method or their scope."[15] Later, when he did study Hindu philosophy, he treated it with the same respect as the Western; all that is suggested here is that he approached Hindu thought from the West.

However, one trait of Ranade's mind was typically Indian, and that was his enthusiasm for religion. "If there has been one feature of our national history which has been its glory and its reward for much suffering, it is the firm belief that 'not what a man hath, but what a man is, or can become', constitutes his real wealth. This is the protest which Indian thought has raised from all time, and which it will continue to raise to the end of time."[16]

Other-worldliness and religious enquiry is almost the only aspect of ancient Indian culture, of which he was really proud. This trait might be traced to his environment in boyhood; religious exultation which he must have experienced at home, in the course of prayers and rituals formed an attitude which could not be eliminated by his subsequent reading.

The intellectual scene which Ranade's wide reading of Western literature presented to him contained many figures and many colours. Greek and Roman cultures, medieval Christian culture, with its other-worldliness, belief in the supernatural, striving for the infinite and frequence of violence, Renaissance humanism rejecting medieval habits of mind, Protestantism, revolting against religious authority of the Roman Catholic Church, Rationalism with its belief that universe works in a rational way and hence is understandable through reason, Enlightenment with its belief that men can, through reason and science, build up a new world in which happiness and perfection could be attained, the nineteenth century with belief in progress strengthened by achievements of natural sciences, and with a variety of social doctrines ranging from Individualism to Socialism—all these passed in review before him as he read, studied and pondered. Out of the numerous strands of Western learning and culture, he had to select and reject. Such was the manner in which Western ideas came to occupy Ranade's thought.

Ranade was a Theist. Theism and Deism were the products of Enlightenment. They were the faiths of those who dismissed from Christianity all that reason which had proved to be wrong, yet who held fast to the idea of God. Ranade who, on one hand, marvelled at the achievements of reason, science and technology in the West, and yet on the other, could not be content with achievements of earthly life, naturally arrived at one of these two faiths. He grasped the underlying principles of Protestantism and theism which he held to be true religion, and then tried to discover them in Hindu religious and philosophical literature. He rejected everything in Hindu religion which was inconsistent with these doctrines. He did not commit himself to reincarnation or to the doctrine of *Karma*, and opposed the caste system which was not altogether unconnected with them. Together with Theism, Ranade believed in the Western doctrine of conscience which is alien to Hindu tradition. Ideas similar to conscience are occasionally found in Hindu literature, such as *dharma* the deity of morality, but on the whole Hindu philosophers do not accept the existence of a separate faculty or kind of reason deciding correctly, what is right and what is wrong. The general Hindu view is that the mind arrives at a decision on this question according to the education it has undergone and only a perfectly developed mind could reach a correct decision.

Several of Ranade's social and political ideas can be traced to theism and the doctrine of conscience, although it is not clear whether, in all cases, Ranade himself was conscious of this logical connection. His conception of social reform was based on conscience, which gave to reformers both the awareness of evils and the strength to defy overwhelming conservatism. The main issue in social reform, he said, was "not this or that particular reform but the general spirit of purity, justice...which should be infused into our minds and which should illuminate our hearts."[17] Exhorting people to break evil customs sanctioned by religious books, he says, "Great and wise men in the past, as in the present, have a claim on our regards, but they must not come between us and our God—the Divine principle enthroned in the heart of everyone of us, high or low... never let this reverence and respect come in the way of the dictates of conscience, the divine command in us."[18] Ranade's attack on *laissez faire* and his plea for extension of State activity both in economic and social affairs is related to his Theism and doctrine of conscience. The philosophy behind *laissez faire* was materialism and individualism; to it Ranade opposed Theistic God who had endowed individuals with conscience, which is but another name for the social nature of man. "It is the higher nature which makes man human, that is his social nature...It is the human part of man's nature, which, in its highest development constitutes his conscience..."[19] Ranade must have held the State to be a product of man's social nature. From this, again follows the view actually expressed by him that the State expresses the best in men. "The State in its collective capacity represents the power, the wisdom, the mercy and charity, of its best citizens."[20] The same doctrines are also behind his view that the State is a moral and an educational institution. He says, "The state after all exists only to make individual members composing it nobler, happier, richer and more perfect, in every attribute with which we are endowed."[21] Ranade's theory of the State was a variant of the Idealistic theory; the metaphysics behind it was not the German or English Idealism but Theism.

Closely connected with Theism and conscience was another characteristically Western idea, namely, Providence, which had more importance in Ranade's political philosophy than is generally believed. When a reference is made to Ranade's frequent suggestions that the British conquest of India was the will of Providence, it is generally thought to be merely a fine phrase, expressing the beneficent nature of the British rule, or at most an expression of an attitude of surrender to the benevolent Almighty, not different from that preached in the *Bhagawad Gita*. Ranade's Providence was seriously meant; and its conception as well as inspiration was distinctly Western. Ranade's Theistic God, immanent as well as transcendent, regulates nature by His Providence, for a great purpose known to Him alone but which surely is benevolent, through laws of physical nature and through the working of conscience in men. The scheme of Providence is a moral government, with its sanctions in the consequences of physical laws and in the discontent of conscience. The scheme is but dimly seen by man by interpreting history intelligently. Ranade often compares the Indian nation with the Jews and, interpreting Indian history, regards Indians too as the chosen race, chosen to be trained through discipline into morally developed and really happy beings. "Change for the better by slow absorption—this has been the characteristic feature of our past history... If the guiding hand of God in history has so favoured us hitherto, why should we despair now when we have been brought under influences of a still more elevating kind?"[22] This conception of Providence and its scheme is clearly Western, closely, connected with the doctrines of Theism and conscience. It is obvious that the conviction of the Providential nature of British rule in India caused Ranade always to put a charitable interpretation on the doings of the British Government. As the conception of Providence made him tolerant of foreign rule, so it made him a gradualist in social reform.

The idea of progress is Western in its origin; it is also recent, modern. It arose and throve in the period of enlightenment in the seventeenth and the eighteenth centuries, and had a firm hold on people's mind in the nineteenth century. Scientific and technological advance which gave birth to it also stirred the imagination of Ranade; and he was infused with the idea of progress and the optimistic spirit. He speaks of "the forces which are at work in the wider world outside and which ... represent all that is best in human efforts for the elevation and happiness of man".[23] Ranade's theory of progress had some distinct characteristics. In the first place, he was somewhat hesitant in his acceptance of this theory. He mentions the achievements of the modern times, not to urge greater achievements, but only to appeal to his countrymen to profit from them and remove their poverty. His Western contemporaries like Spencer, not only realised the immense significance of progress but were glowing with optimism, dwelling on the limitless possibilities for the future of humanity, and this note of exhilaration is missing in Ranade's writings. Ranade could not forget that he was an Indian; and India had not shared the achievements of science and technology. In the second place, to Ranade, retrogression is as important a phenomenon as progress. All advocates of this theory note that progress is not continuous and that there are epochs of retrogression; but Ranade is unique in feeling greatly concerned with retrogression. He says, "The theory of evolution has in this country, to be studied in its other aspect of what may conveniently be called devolution".[24] Here, too, Ranade's concern with India is evident. The third characteristic of Ranade's view of progress is his emphasis on the moral aspect. Among Western thinkers, the theory of progress, which began as one relating to knowledge, afterwards expanded into a general theory, and then it emphasised its material side. To Ranade, however, the essence of progress lay in the sphere of religion and morality. "The evolution that we should seek is a change from constraint to freedom—constraint imposed by our own weaker nature over the freedom of our higher powers." Lastly, Ranade refuted the notion, implied in many interpretations of this theory such as those of Condorcet, Comte and Hegel, that, Oriental nations like India could not hope to progress. Some of the wisest of them

(Europeans) have demonstrated to their own satisfaction that all oriental races have had their day .... Happily for us these prophecies are not true, and what is more, it is in our power to falsify them."[25]

As pointed out earlier, that other worldliness was a typically Indian trait in Ranade's thought. And yet in this respect also Ranade could not escape the influence of the West. On the whole, the West has attached great value to good life here on earth. It is true that Indians in ancient times, far from neglecting things of this world, were leading other civilisations in science, technology, trade and social organisation; it is also true that in the West, the ascetic ideal was held up by medieval Christianity, and it is only after the industrial revolution that the worldliness of the West became pronounced. Yet it is a safe generalisation to make that the East laid stress on other-worldliness and asceticism, and the West did the opposite. Under the influence of the East, the dominant interest for Ranade was in religion and other-worldliness; but under the influence of the West Ranade was, firstly, enthusiastic about removing poverty through technological and economic progress, and secondly, was opposed to the traditional admiration of asceticism in India. He is for a balanced view on this matter. "The Theist believes that the practice of austerities and the virtues of ascetic life defeats the main end of our existence in this world. It deprives us of the education and discipline of self-government, which living in society has a tendency to foster in us. At the same time, in a society too much given up to self-indulgence and luxury the example of men (spending their life) in the practice of poverty, chastity and austerities, is good as a protest."[26] It is this balanced view which left ample room for material well-being. It made him turn his able mind to the study of economic science, and to earnest endeavours to raise the standard of living of the masses.

Doctrines of Theism and conscience, the concept of Providence, the idea of progress, and the Western attachment to good things of this world as a corrective to Eastern stress on matters of the spirit, then, were the important streams of Western influence on Ranade's thought. But of greater importance than all these was the Western method of study and thinking. Intent on finding the root cause of the amazing superiority of the West in respect of material wealth, moral qualities and intellectual attainments, he traced back the history of Western culture to the point where the two cultures and their levels were not basically different, namely, the end of the medieval age; and, tracing the steps of cultural progress of the West from this point, he came to the conclusion that freedom from authority, reliance on reason, testing of intuitive truths by individual's own experience, observation and experimentation, comparison and induction, were the thinking methods or techniques which made the West what it was in his day. At an early age, in 1861, he wrote about ancient Indian thinkers: "They are diametrically opposed to Bacon's method and are full of the restless agitation and the dogmatic tendency which Bacon has censured. They despise that knowledge of nature which they derive from observation as being low and sordid. They have recourse to mental abstraction and contemplation and spun a web out of their brains which astounds us all and is intelligible to none." Unfair as this judgement is, it shows how keen Ranade was on abandoning what he supposed to be the methods of ancient Indian thinkers and on adopting Western techniques. He was enamoured of what was then the latest and the most advanced methods of studying social questions, namely, the historical and the comparative methods. He deftly applied them in his studies in Indian social customs, Indian economics, and Indian administrative problems. Among the conclusions he reached by these methods are: (a) "Internal dissensions, the upheaval of non-Aryan, and the predominance acquired by barbarous Scythian and Mohammedan conquerors degraded the condition of the female sex (in India)." (b) In 1893, there were good grounds for the hope that India had entered on the path of industrialisation; but it was necessary for Indian industries to work up our raw materials a stage further before they were exported and import more raw produce from abroad to be worked up here. (c) Between 1875 and 1880, famine and riots dominated administrative discussions, and the root cause of the riots were the high rates of land revenue.[27]

Ranade's utterings is seen as a reflection of the Western sentiment of nationalism. It is not aggressive nationalism, not even nationalism demanding independence. It is cultural and humanitarian nationalism. It is possible he got it from Herder, who believed that the greatness of Jewish nationalism lay in 'its ethical aspirations and spiritual unity'. Ranade's nationalism may be described as the internationally minded nationalism of a leader who believes in the elevating effect of the contact with a morally superior conquering country. Ranade is "conscious of a background of common traditions, common religion, common laws and institutions and customs and perversions of such customs... in spite of our differences." He comes nearest to nationalistic pride when he speaks of 'the nobility of our common stock and ancient origin' and proceeds to point out that 'most of the social evils complained of in these days were unknown in the days of our highest glory'. But the element of nationalism that was strong in his mind was a constructive and creative aspiration for the future: "With a liberated manhood, with buoyant hope, with a faith that never shirks duty, with a sense of justice that deals fairly to all, with unclouded intellect and powers fully cultivated, and, lastly, with a love that overleaps all bounds, renovated India will take her proper rank among the nations of the world, and be the master of the situation and of her own destiny."[28]

REFERENCES

1. Panikkar, K.M., *Asia and Western Dominance* (London: George Allen and Unwin). 1964, p. 154.
2. Jagirdar, P. J., *Studies in the Social Thought of M.G. Ranade, op. cit.*, p. 12.
3. Javedkar, S.D., *Adhunik Bharat* (Pune: Sadashiv), 1947, pp. 10-11.
4. Ibid., p. 54.
5. Singh, Gurumukh N., *Indian Constitutional and National Development* (Ajmer: Sachin), 1959, p. 105.
6. Gadgil, D.R., *Industrial Evolution of India* (Delhi: Oxford University Press), 1959.
7. *Ibid.*, p. 60.
8. Bury, J. B., *History of the Freedom of Thought* (London: Oxford University Press), 1960, pp. 127-128.
9. Panikkar, *K.M., Asia and Western Dominance, op. cit.*, p. 39.
10. Sen, J.M., *History of Elementary Education in India* (Calcutta: Suptd. Government and Printing), 1917, p. 35
11. Panikkar, K.M., *Asia and Western Dominance, op. cit.*
12. Jagirdar, P.J., *Studies in the Social Thought of M.G. Ranade, op. cit.*, p. 25.
13. Panikkar, K.M., *Asia and Western Dominance, op. cit.*, p. 317.

14. Kabir, Humayun, *The Indian Heritage* (Bombay: Bharatiya Vidya Bhawan), 1953, p. 119.
15. Jagirdar, P.J., *Studies in the Social Thought of M.G. Ranade, op. cit.*, p. 99.
16. Ranade, M. G., *Religious and Social Reforms* (New Delhi: Sahitya Akademi), 1992, pp. 2-3.
17. Ranade, Ramabai, *Miscellaneous Writings of the Late Hon'ble Mr. Justice M.G. Ranade, op. cit.*, p. 212.
18. *Ibid.*, p. 194.
19. *Ibid.*, p. 68.
20. *Ibid.*, p. 78.
21. *Ibid.*, p. 172.
22. *Ibid.*, p. 126.
23. *Ibid.*, p. 246.
24. Ranade, M.G., *Religious and Social Reforms, op. cit.*, p. 27.
25. Ranade, Ramabai, *Miscellaneous Writings of the Late Hon'ble Mr. Justice M.G. Ranade, op. cit.*, p. 115.
26. Ranade, M.G., *Religious and Social Reforms, op. cit.*, p. 271.
27. Ranade, Ramabai, *Miscellaneous Writings of the Late Hon'ble Mr. Justice M.G. Ranade, op. cit.*, p. 76.
28. *Ibid.*, pp: 89-90, 179.

3

THE THEORY OF THE STATE

Ranade never gave a systematic exposition of a theory of the State. There was, however, a coherence in his political views on various questions which implies the existence of such a theory, whether consciously held or not. Ranade's theory of the State is thus to be seen not directly but in its reflection in his writings and speeches.

The origins of Ranade's political thought are to be found, firstly, in the prevailing conditions of national life in India, and secondly, in the Western political tradition of liberalism. That India was in a condition of political subjection was, in the opinion of thinkers like Ranade, but a superficial view. In his boyhood, Ranade in a school essay, once expressed 'pain' because 'our former power and glory have departed from our nation'[1]; but his writings or speeches rarely deal with this theme. Seen in the historical perspective, India's condition was distinctly better than what it was for several centuries past; politically it was much better, socially a little better, and economically it promised to be better. This improvement in the condition was the direct result of the contact of the British people who at the moment were far more advanced in every respect. The high level of civilization which the British had attained showed the possibilities before India if only she seized the opportunity. And it seemed to be the duty, if not the destined role, of the English-educated class to which Ranade belonged to be the instrument of an immense cultural upheaval. This situation set limits to any theory of the state which Ranade could hold—the theory must not imply that foreign rule in itself is an evil.

The second main source was the political tradition of Western liberalism. Ranade saw that if India were to progress, she must seek inspiration from the West. As he studied Western literature, he learnt that political liberalism, growth of sciences, technological development, rational outlook, were all closely interconnected. Liberalism was thus the political aspect of an advanced culture. However, Ranade was attracted by one element of pre-liberal medieval European culture, namely, the religious fervour involving the moral standpoint, intellectual humility, and resort to faith as a valuable means of obtaining knowledge. Within the liberal tradition, Ranade was one of those who strongly reacted against the extreme materialism and extreme individualism of the Utilitarians. In England the doctrine of such thinkers was Idealism. Ranade too was an Idealist; but it is doubtful whether he owed anything to English Idealists.

The essential ideas of the liberal tradition are individual freedom, supremacy of the law of reason, constitutional government and participation in political life as a necessary means of realising freedom. Individual freedom had, it is true, its origin in the Christian concept of the supreme worth of the individual; but Reformation, by destroying the concept of the intervening hierarchy of priesthood between an individual and God, endowed a greater significance to the individual personality; and as Renaissance led the individual to discover his powers of creation and, of initiative, individual autonomy came to be emphasised for the fuller realisation of the individual's potentialities. Liberalism, thus, makes individual freedom its goal; it is its major premise. But all individuals must recognise some authority; and the only authority consistent with freedom is the authority of law, impersonal, free from caprice, and objective. Law as supreme authority, had to be conceived as rational, universal and eternal. But law, the supremacy of which guaranteed individual freedom, had to be conceived as the product of individual will as well as the embodiment of values transcending individual will. These are contradictory notions; for, how is it certain that individuals will not will that which is against general interest? To solve this contradiction liberalism acknowledges one, and only one, limitation on the individual will, namely that of individual conscience.

Conscience, thus, is 'the Keystone of the whole liberal structure.'[2] Constitutional government is the practical political expression of liberalism; it implies the establishment of effective political means of control whereby the rule of law may be enforced. The fourth essential idea was the necessity of participation in organised political life for the realisation of freedom. This last idea, however, was slow in its development. Ranade's political thought is deeply impressed by these ideas.

Being an Idealist, Ranade's political thought rested on his views on Religion and Metaphysics, even as Hobbes' had rested on Physics, or Spencer's on Biology. On Philosophy Ranade has written essays which clearly show the system he believes in. Between his Philosophy of which we have clear knowledge and his casual general remarks illuminating discussions of political, social and economic questions of the day, there lies a political theory. As said above, it is difficult to say whether he consciously held it; but it did give coherence to his views on a variety of problems.

Spiritual Life and Worldly Life

Religious outlook, in some religious faiths, implies the view that life of the spirit is real life and that life of the body is at best irrelevant and at worst a hindrance to spiritual life. There is a notion that this view was characteristic of Eastern faiths, though it is difficult to reconcile it with the vigorous economic and political life which prevailed in ancient and medieval India for thousands of years. Yet the notion that India was indifferent to worldly life was common among enlightened men both in India and England. Those who hold the view of the meaninglessness of the life of the body do not need any science of economics, politics or sociology. Such indeed was the position of some reflective Greek thinkers in the period after the loss of political freedom; they had a tendency to deny the importance of worldly affairs. Christianity, however, inherited the tradition of the Jews who were concerned with the spiritual significance of worldly existence. The Jews believed that events of history are themselves a part of God's universal purpose, and that man's spiritual duty is not to escape from the world but to conduct his life in such a way as to further the divine plan.[3] This view was absorbed in Christianity. The Christian road to salvation consisted, not in renouncing the world but in using one's life as an occasion for responsible conduct. In this form the view became part of the tradition of Western thought. Ranade took it over from the West. It is seen in his conceptions of Providence and Conscience. It is clearly seen in his remark: "The practice of austerities and virtues of ascetic life defeats the main end of our existence in this world. It deprives us of the education and discipline of self-government, which living in society has a tendency to foster in us."[4]

This view of reality of life opens the way to thought about economic, social and political life. However, it indicates a purpose to which life of this world should be directed; further, it also postulates a spiritual force which acts unseen for the ultimate good of all. Both the purposes of life as well as the force which works for the fulfilment of it emanate not from experience of senses, but from the mind. This makes clear that Ranade is to be placed among the Idealist thinkers in social and political thought. "When mind itself is made the object of knowledge, one becomes capable of discriminating between good and evil. This faculty is called *Viveka* or *Vijnana* ... *Vijnana* is the basis of morality, law, politics and household arrangements."[5]

Freedom

Ranade's conception of liberty or freedom originates from a certain conception of the purpose of human life which in its turn, is the outcome of his metaphysical views summarised earlier. The nature and purpose of life may be stated in Ranade's own words: "Our present state of existence is one of trial and preparation, a state of probation and discipline in virtue and piety, qualifying us for a future sphere of existence." "Difficulties, temptations and dangers, require in us habits of self-denial and discipline, and submission to present pain for future pleasure; our present state is therefore, one not merely of trial, but of discipline also." And what is the 'future sphere of existence' for which discipline is the preparation? It is salvation of the soul, which Ranade describes thus: "When the human soul ...

acquires habits which enable it, while in the body or on leaving the body to escape its trammels and its lusts, to enter into more intimate relation with God, and realise vividly the blessings of God's presence and holiness ... this consummation of the soul is salvation."[6]

There is, in every individual, a force which impels him to attain this goal through self-discipline. That force is the moral sense, which in its developed form is called conscience. "We are endowed with the capacity of improving ourselves by experience and the growth of active and passive habits, which inculcate self-government, as the practical principle of all virtue and pious submission to God's will."[7] An individual is a soul... There are as many souls as there are human beings"—which Ranade describes as "a spirit...not a form or activity of matter as physically understood," and as having mental and moral capacities, the individual's soul is immortal.

With this view of the individual and the purpose of his life, it is easy to see that liberty can only mean a man's moral and spiritual development, the development of all the faculties and capacities in the direction of salvation of the soul, without hindrance from any side. The most serious hindrance comes from certain elements within oneself. This is Ranade's theory of liberty or freedom. Accordingly, Ranade once said: "The evolution we should seek is a change from constraint to freedom—constraint imposed by our own weaker nature over (to?) the freedom of our higher powers".[8] Essentially, freedom means, freedom of our higher powers, unhindered by lower elements of man's nature. But this process involves the putting of restraints on these lower elements. Even where Ranade intends to oppose social restraints of an immoral character, he defines liberation as "change from the restraints of family and caste customs to the self-imposed restraints of the free will of the individual."[9] Freedom is freedom of the moral will of an individual. It is not freedom of will seeking the objects of any desire. Man's lower nature tempts him into pursuit of desires of lower order; his higher nature beckons him to do his duty; he is free when he can, and, does, do his duty in spite of temptations. Man alone is capable of freedom, for he alone possesses the capacity to choose between right and wrong.[10] Freedom, he says, should be 'responsible to the voice of God in us.'[11] This view of freedom is very much similar to Kant's. Kant interprets freedom as the right to will a self-imposed imperative of duty. According to Kant, we have our 'empirical Self' which is but a creature of desire, which is subject to the law of cause and effect determining our actions so long as they are determined by our desires; and besides it, there is another Self, the moral or 'transcendental self' that is capable of legislating for itself. It is this Self which is free. In deciding how we should act, we have to transcend the realm of what is determined by our desires and act in terms of some principle prescribing how we ought to act. It is in the act of deciding to do this rather than that, that we experience freedom. The first part of Ranade's definition of freedom as the elimination of 'constraint imposed by our weaker nature' is not different from Kant's view that we must transcend the realm of what is determined by our desires, and the second part of his definition of freedom as 'the freedom of our higher powers' seems identical with Kant's view that we are free when we ourselves decide, subduing our empirical self, to do this rather than that, because to do this is in accordance with what we ought to do. "Acting in accordance with the idea of moral law," says Kant, "he acts in accordance with the law of his being. Only then is he free, only then does he transcend the world of cause and effect."[12]

It is legitimate to infer from this view of liberty as a moral concept that Ranade regarded society and the State as meaningful only because of their contribution to moral freedom. Freedom in the context of society and of the State can only be defined in terms of this contribution. Ranade does hold that this contribution is substantial. Individual life directed to its real purpose of salvation means exercising the faculty of *viveka, vijnana*, or conscience, the faculty of discriminating between right and wrong. Society gives fuller scope, which solitude does not, for the exercising of this faculty—to use his words, society has a tendency to foster discipline of self-government. Household arrangements or the social code has its basis in this *vijnana*. Social life has its organised form, and in that form society is the State. The State too must foster the discipline of self-government and must make and enforce a legal code which is favourable to it. According to Ranade, law also is based on *vijnana.* Liberty in the text of society means a social atmosphere favourable to life according to the dictates of conscience; liberty in the context of the State means the legal and political atmosphere favourable to life according to the dictates of conscience. Such is the theory of liberty implied in Ranade's writings.

The close resemblance of this theory with that of Green suggests that Ranade might have taken it from him. This is possible, but not certain. There are certain points in favour of this possibility. Green's works were published in 1883, and Ranade was likely to have read them. Moreover, Green dominated the academic world of his time, On the other hand, if Ranade had read and adopted Green's theory of freedom, he would have mentioned it somewhere in an approving manner, as he did in the case of the historical school of economics. Secondly, Ranade nowhere uses Green's particular terminology. Green worked out his theory of freedom and of the functions of the State—carefully and elaborately—which Ranade never did. Ranade hints at a theory; Green independently states the same theory, and develops and refines it. What seems probable is that similarity of approach, that is, a strong reaction against extreme individualism and, materialism of Utilitarians, is responsible for the similarity of broad conclusions of both Green and Ranade; the latter probably read Green but Green's writings were far from his mind when he made the observations implying that theory.

The pre-liberal medieval religious fervour is seen in the insistence that morality is based on the God-given capacity for discriminating between good and evil, and that the function of this capacity, or conscience, is to lead the soul to its salvation. The essential ideas of liberalism are also seen in some form or the other. Freedom is freedom for the individual; though it is conceived as moral freedom, the restraints implied in it are to be imposed by the individual himself and not by any outside authority. The design of God is conveyed to men through the conscience within and not through priesthood. "The turn of life and light is in the individual. We have to purify it to feel the heat and the light of truth in us."[13] "Never let this reverence and respect for prophets and revelations come in the way of the dictates of conscience."[14] The State also, he said, "exists only to make individual members composing it nobler, happier, richer and more perfect."[15] Defining 'faith' as 'practical reason' and thus never contrary to it, Ranade consistently stood for the autonomy of individual reason; he made it the basis of his plea for social reform, in spite of seemingly adverse religious texts and for the liberty of changing ones religious faith. Supremacy of the law of reason is seen in Ranade's emphasis on conscience, which according to Hallowell, is the 'keystone of the whole liberal structure'.

Ranade's idealistic reaction against materialism and extreme individualism of the Utilitarians is clearly seen in his theory of liberty. As against materialism, Ranade made spiritual development and suppression of temptations the very essence of liberty; and as against extreme individualism, Ranade stated that it was the social nature of man which was his higher nature, and it was the triumph of this higher nature over the lower which constituted liberty.

The Purpose and the Nature of the State

It is legitimate to infer from the above discussion that Ranade's view about freedom is prior to the state. Freedom is prior to society as well as the State. Freedom in the sense of unhindered moral development of all individuals is the purpose to which society and the State make their contribution, and they derive their value from their contribution to this end. "The State after all exists only to make individual members composing it nobler, happier, richer and more perfect, in every attribute with which we are endowed." At the same time the State and society—and within society, economic, literary and artistic life—are spheres in which development of capacities, which is freedom, is to be attained. This second aspect of the role of the State is set forth by him in the following passage: "Whether in the political, or social or religious, or commercial, or manufacturing or aesthetical spheres, in literature, in science, in art, in war, in peace, it is the individual and collective man who has to develop his powers.

Although Ranade distinguished between society and the State, he attributed to both of them the same purpose. Aristotle who did not make the distinction said that the State exists to make life good; Hegel made that distinction and yet held that in the State the personality realises moral development or freedom, while civil society is incapable of the task. The task according to Ranade is essentially that of the individual impelled from within by the Divine faculty or conscience; he is only aided in his efforts by society as well as the State.

What, according to Ranade, is the distinction between the State and society? The fact that he regards both to have the same ultimate purpose indicates that the distinction is not vital. At one place he actually eliminated it altogether; he refers to the 'collective humanity we call the society or State'. The distinctions where he does make it, is therefore a minor one. It appears to lie in the mode of action adopted by the 'collective humanity'. Here, once again, is an area of Ranade's thought on which his observations throw only an indirect light. Mere logical inference lead to the conclusion that he held the following view. When the 'collective humanity' acts through a concrete organisation we call government or administration and when it uses the sanction of force behind its law, it is the State. A careful reading of his 'Introduction', to Mr. Vaidya's Book shows that Ranade does not treat 'society' as an entity capable of acting. There is the State, and there are individuals acting voluntarily, who may be termed society. "The first objection urged on this head is that there are social questions which is not the duty of the State to regulate. We answer that this argument is not open to those who welcome as the vast majority of this class of opponents freely acknowledge state regulation of Sati and widow marriage ... Individual liberty of action is no doubt a great force, but this liberty has its limitation imposed by the fact that no man's liberty should encroach upon the liberty of those who surround him ... What a single man, or a combination of men, can best do on their amount, that the State may not do ..."[16] (It may be noticed that in the above passage, Ranade uses the word 'liberty' in the current sense of non-interference by the State, and not in accordance with his own interpretation of the concept). Ranade equates 'society' with 'individuals' by using the words synonymously.

Concerted action of the 'collective humanity' which may be called 'society or the State' can only be taken by the State. And probably it is for this reason that Ranade has a higher opinion of the

State than of unorganised individuals. He appears to think that mobilisation and organisation of men automatically results in the mobilisation of physical force, intellectual talents and moral capabilities. Thus alone can be explained the very high regard he has for the State, as expressed in his statement: "The State in its collective capacity represents the power, the wisdom, the mercy and charity, of its best citizens."[17]

His regard for the State is thus very high, somewhat higher than Green who might not have agreed with this statement. Ranade never takes up the Hegelian position; he remains a liberal. For, according to Hegel, God or the World-Spirit finds its highest expression in the State and individual's freedom consists in acting in conformity to the will of the State; while, according to Ranade, God expresses himself, however imperfectly, through the consciences of individuals; and though the State is greater because it represents the consciences of its best individual citizens, liberty consists in their moral development, depending primarily on their own activity guided by the conscience of each.

The basis of the State is not force, but will, although Ranade does not express it in these words: "The wisdom, the mercy and charity of its best citizens"—note the word 'best'—is, in essence, not different from the 'common will' of Kant, the 'rational will' of Fichte and the 'goodwill' of Green. In particular, Ranade's conception of the basis of the State resembles that of Green. Green conceives of will as "the will and reason of men as determined by social relations, as interested in each other acting together for common ends. It is a power which this universal rational will exercises over the inclinations of the individual and which only needs exceptionally to be backed by coercive force."[18]

It would not be wrong to identify Ranade's 'wisdom, mercy and charity of the best citizens of the State' with Green's 'will and reason of men as interested in each other' and with his 'universal rational will'; and throughout all his writings, Ranade gives a subordinate place to force as a factor supporting the State.

That the Indian State was ruled by foreigners did not prevent Ranade from applying this concept of the State to it. It is a characteristic of Idealist thinkers that they do not necessarily believe that the general will of the State can only find expression in a democratically elected legislature or executive. Kant held that sovereign general will was capable of being expressed through one person. Green would call any determinate superior to the sovereign "upon condition that behind that superior, determining his and inspiring his acts, is recognised the general will." Ranade likewise seems to have thought that in his general will, the common conscience, the common conviction that makes for righteousness, as Green puts it, stood behind the British Government in India. Or rather, the British Government sensed the general will in India better than their predecessors and allowed themselves to be influenced by it, except possibly when the interests of England clashed with those of India. Dealing with the objection that the State should not legislate, or interfere with social matters, because the government is foreign, Ranade says, "In this case, however, the foreign rulers have no interest to move over their own accord ... The initiation is to be ours."[19]

There is sure to be a very large area in day-to-day administration where the interests of the foreign rulers do not conflict with the interests of the people, and therefore, on the whole, exposed to the moral sense, or the wisdom, of the best citizens. Ranade had actual experience of this influence, for he was both an administrator of justice as well as an active public man. The wisdom and the spirit of service of Indian citizens, Ranade must have observed, had more influence with the British Government in India than with the preceding Indian governments, numerous and aggrandising, stalking the land since about the middle of the eighteenth century. Ranade's grandfather and father as dutiful servants, and Ranade himself as a responsible officer, were part and parcel of the governmental organisation which cast a benign influence in all directions.

The British had conquered India by force and fraudulent diplomacy and yet the British Government in its working was benevolent. In this, Ranade evidently saw that there was something in the State as an institution which tends to make it subservient to the best thoughts and convictions of the people of a country, whatever be its form of government, and whether it be foreign or national.

Law and the State

Ranade's concept of law, as expressed in his published writings, bears the imprint of the historical school of jurisprudence. The historical jurists conceived of laws as determined by characteristics and experiences of a particular people. It is widely known that Ranade held economic truths to be relative to the characteristics of the social life of a nation; but it has escaped the attention of his commentators that he held the doctrine of relativity in respect of jurisprudence also. This is not surprising, because the influence of the historical school on his writings on the legal aspect of society is not so obvious.

One reason for the obscurity of this influence is that generally the historical school jurists tended to be conservative and Ranade was a reformer. The general implication of the historical conception of law is that reform is impossible and that it is better to allow the historical process, to work out itself without hindrance. Ranade did not deduce this inference from it. He held that behind all historical processes in different societies there was a benevolent force working for righteousness, acting through conscience of individuals; and changes in the course of history can be accounted for, partly by the strengthening or weakening of this force in individuals in particular societies.

The influence of the historical school on Ranade can be seen in his doctrine of continuity of social life of a particular society. There is something organic about a society, and a radical change will injure it. "There are those among us who think that, in this connection, the work of the reformer is confined only to a brave resolve to break with the past, and do what our individual reason suggests, as proper and fit. The power of long-formed habits and tendencies is, however, ignored in this view of the matter ... While respecting the past, we must ever seek to correct the parasitic growth that have encrusted it (our society) and sucked the life out of it."[20] This implies that each particular society has a life of its own, capable of forming habits (or at least instilling its members with habits), and capable also of adopting habits that are suicidal. This 'life' of a particular society, in its turn, implies a national mind that reveals itself in the orderly practices of national community in which the historical jurists believe. The only point of doubt here is whether Ranade thought that law should do no more than register the decisions of this mind, that 'enacted law should be only a formal embodiment of historic law'. This doubt can be dispelled by a close scrutiny of his writings. Ranade's plea for some reformist social legislation was based on three grounds, firstly that 'State regulation represents the highest and most disinterested wisdom of times', that 'the state, in its collective capacity represents the power, the wisdom, the mercy and charity of its best citizens', secondly, that the initiation in the legislative process is taken by leaders of the particular society concerned, and, thirdly, that, the proposed legislation seeks a change "as a return and restoration to the days of our past history". Thus the plea was for translating the best will and the best institutions of India into law. A clear evidence of Ranade's acceptance of the historical school is the following passage in this same connection:

> "It is further argued, in deprecation of State action, that in this matter we must not lose sight of the fact that institutions, like constitutions, must grow and cannot be made to conform with foreign ideals to order. There is, no doubt, some force in this observation, and it would be a fatal objection if the argument for change were based on the ground that we must copy the foreign exemplar."[21]

In particular, Ranade was influenced by Sir Henry Sumner Maine, the classic exponent of the historical school of jurisprudence in England. Maine, from his study of ancient laws and institutions, came to the conclusion that the main line of human evolution was from a condition of status, in which the position of the individual was determined by membership in his group, to one of contract, in which the position of the individual was determined by his own choice. He believed that freedom of contract was the end towards which society moved. Compare with this view the following remark of Ranade: "The change which we should all seek is thus a change from constraint to freedom, from credulity to faith, from status to contract ... This is what I understand by social evolution."[22] Quite in harmony with this historical jurisprudence is Ranade's view that social development in every sphere is dependent on development in every other sphere, because in this respect society is like an organism, having life and growth as its attributes. Savigny, one of the earliest exponents of the historical school of jurisprudence, found the spirit of the people embodied in law, just as others found it embodied in popular songs, fairy-tales and language. That each nation is a spirit of which its literature, science, morals and laws are expressions is also the suggestion in the following passage from Ranade's writings: " Whether in the political, or social, or religious, or commercial, or manufacturing on aesthetical spheres, in literature, independence, in art, in war, in peace, it is the individual, who has to develop his powers by his own exertions. You cannot have a good social system when you find yourself low in the scale of political rights, nor can you be fit to exercise political rights and privileges, unless your social system is based on reason and justice. You cannot have a good commercial system when your social arrangements are imperfect."[23]

In adopting the view of law of the historical school, Ranade was not departing from his Idealistic philosophy. His conception of God as a moral governor "in no way conflicts with the voluntary and limited freedom of man's activities"[24] and in different nations men may choose different types of behaviour and morals. God's law concerning men is only the general law of morality enforced through such conscience as men possess; but men are free to choose and free to act or not according to conscience. God's law of nature is but a force in human affairs, succeeding in the end but allowing men freedom of action. The historical school of jurisprudence itself was influenced by Idealism. Roscoe Pound describes the relation between the two schools thus: Both the philosophical and historical schools "postulated an ideal law. One sought to discover this ideal law through history, the other sought to find it through logical development of an abstract form,...Philosopher and historian were agreed that law was found not made."[25] Hallowell says, "Each supplemented the other. From metaphysical deductions one found the form of law, from history the content of law."[26] According to

Dean Pound, Sir Henry Maine, one of the members of the historical school, is at bottom Hegelian."[27]

Between ideal law discovered through history and ideal law found through reasoning, Ranade regarded the latter as possessing greater force and validity. Laws of a nation, like its social customs, religion, literature, science and art, tend to express the spirit which gives life to a nation; but this spirit itself is moved by an all-pervading eternal force making for righteousness. This is clearly his view underlying his following observation: "Above all mere ordinances and institutes stands the law eternal, of justice and equality, of pity and compassion, the suggestions of conscience within and of nature without us. We can no more resist the stream of these influences as working for righteousness than we can roll back the tide. All real prudence would dictate that we should take full measure of these influences and decide how far we must accommodate ourselves to the inevitable."[28]

In the matter of social customs and institutions, Ranade advises ardent reformers to exercise prudence and not to attempt to break with the past, and on the other hand, he advises the conservatives to exercise prudence and not to attempt to resist the stream of these influences as working for righteousness, the stream coming not from history but from the ever present eternity. Ranade's passionate plea for gradual reform is thus based on his integration of the principles of the historical and the idealistic schools.

We can conclude that there are three features of Ranade's thoughts on society and the State. In the first place, his observations on various kinds of problems current in his day were locally connected with each other, so that a single system of thought held them together. Secondly, Ranade's whole thought was dominated by his views on religion and metaphysics. Thirdly, Ranade was a thinker in the Western tradition, although very greatly concerned with ameliorating Indian conditions—political, economic, social and religious.

The economic ideas of Ranade were linked with his ideas on political theory; and these, in turn, were related to his metaphysical and religious ideas. The central thought in his economic writings was a plea for vigorous State activity; and what enabled him to entertain this thought was his idealism in political theory which regards the State as a friend. This relation between his economic and political ideas has not received attention, partly because his own arguments in support of this plea were only economic, such as his attack on the classical school from the standpoint of the historical school of economics, and his reliance on List. It is possible that Ranade himself was not conscious of this relationship. Perhaps he was not conscious even of his belonging to the Idealist school of political thought; for, he was independently developing his thoughts, mainly on the foundation of Kant's philosophy. His arguments in economic writings showed him as belonging to the historical school; analysis in this work shows that he belonged to the historical school not only in respect of economics but also in respect of law. His adherence to the historical school did not conflict with his Idealistic political thought; there were other thinkers also who combined the historical with the Idealistic view. His Idealistic political theory flowed from his Idealism in metaphysics and religion. He, therefore, attacked the classical school not only in respect of their economic ideas of *laissez faire*, but also of their political ideas of individualism and of their metaphysical ideas of materialism. The optimism and the enthusiasm which pervaded his economic, political and social reformist writings were generated by his religious and metaphysical doctrines of God, Providence, faith and conscience. Thus his thoughts in all the departments of knowledge were interconnected, as usually happens with powerful minds.

That Ranade's system of social thought was dominated by his metaphysical ideas can be seen from the fact that several of his ideas flow directly or indirectly from his convictions about faith, God, Providence and Conscience. In his opinion, in the long run social reform implying abolition of inhuman customs is inevitable, because above all ordinances and social codes, there is eternal law of justice, compassion and love. Evolution, to Ranade, means moral progress, and this view follows from his religious conviction that God is the moral governor of all human souls for attaining freedom from the trammels and lusts of the body. Ranade equates the social nature of man with his divine nature, meaning thereby that God, out of benevolence, has implanted in human heart the impulse to live with others in society, and this conviction placed him with the Idealists and against the Materialist Utilitarian Individualists in political and economic theory. This line of thinking also made him define the purpose of the State as to make men, not only richer and happier, but also nobler. God, he held, presided over history, so that the British conquest of India was, for the ultimate welfare of both India and England, and not the result of a mere competitive struggle in which the strong enslaved the weak. These are but few instances to show that many of Ranade's ideas on social questions, and especially those on the central problems of social and political theory, were intimately connection with, if not flowed from his distinctive metaphysical ideas.

Ranade's mind was saturated with Western thought. He adopted the historical and the comparative method in vogue in Western social sciences. For the metaphysical foundations of his social thought he is largely indebted to Kant, from whom he took over his conceptions of faith, conscience and freedom. The structure of social and political theory which Ranade built on these foundations is hidden from the public view because Ranade never wrote a systematic book on theory; but from such glimpses of it as are available through his discussions of current problems, one can see that its nature was the same as that of Idealism. It was variant of Idealism which was not as developed in Germany by Fischte and Hegel, but as in England by Green. Ranade probably developed it independently of Green; and this supports the conjecture that Ranade did not owe anything to him. But Ranade was as eager as Green to refute the Utilitarian Individualism of the mid-nineteenth century England; or, while in Green's country it proved inadequate to meet the challenge of the 'condition-of-England question', it also failed to solve the Indian counterpart of that question, namely the destruction of domestic industries and increased pressure of population on land consequent upon competition of manufactured goods imported from abroad. Even as Ranade attacked the modern Western materialistic tradition of Bentham and Mill, the first inspiration of spiritualism came to him not from Hinduism but from Protestantism and Theism of the West, and it was only later than he discovered similar appealing doctrines preached in the course of the religious history of India. Ranade was thus essentially a thinker in the Western tradition.

REFERENCES

1. Jagirdar, P. J., *Studies in the Social Thought of M.G. Ranade, op. cit.*, p. 81.
2. Hallowell, G.H., *Modern Currents Political Thought* (New York: Holt), 1953, p. 91.
3. Watkins, F., *The Political Tradititons of the West* (London: Nelson), 1953.
4. Ranade, M.G., *Religious and Social Reforms, op. cit.*, p. 273.
5. Jagirdar, P.J., *Studies in the Social Thought of M.G. Ranade, op. cit.*, p. 84.
6. Ranade, M.G., *Religious and Social Reforms, op. cit.*, p. 271.
7. *Ibid.*, p. 266.
8. Ranade, *Ramabai, Miscellaneous Writings of the Late Hon'ble Mr. Justice M.G. Ranade, op. cit.*, p. 116.
9. *Ibid.*, p. 82.
10. Ranade, M.G., *Religious and Social Reforms, op. cit.*, p. 20.
11. Ranade, Ramabai, *Miscellaneous Writings of the Late Hon'ble Mr. Justice M.G. Ranade, op. cit.*, p. 194.
12. Hallowell, G.H., *Modern Currents Political Thought, op. cit.*, p. 246.
13. *Ibid.*, p. 172.
14. Ranade, Ramabai, *Miscellaneous Writings of the Late Hon'ble Mr. Justice M.G. Ranade, op. cit.*, p. 42.
15. *Ibid.*, p. 194.
16. *Ibid.*, p. 78.
17. *Ibid.*
18. Green, T.H., *Principles of Political Obligations* (London: Allen and Unwin), 1934, p. 103.
19. *Ibid.*, pp. 90-91.
20. Ranade, Ramabai, *Miscellaneous Writings of the Late Hon'ble Mr. Justice M.G. Ranade, op. cit.*, p. 118.
21. Ranade, M.G., *Religious and Social Reforms, op. cit.*, p. 107.
22. Ranade, Ramabai, *Miscellaneous Writings of the Late Hon'ble Mr. Justice M.G. Ranade, op. cit.*, pp. 116-17.
23. *Ibid.*, p. 231.
24. Ranade, M.G., *Religious and Social Reforms, op. cit.*, pp. 265-66.
25. Pound, Roscoe, *Spirit of Common Law* (New York: Yale University Press), 1955, pp. 153-154.
26. Hallowell, G.H., *Modern Political Thought, op. cit.*
27. Jagirdar, P.J., *Studies in the Social Thought of M.G. Ranade, op. cit.*, p. 94.
28. Ranade, Ramabai, *Miscellaneous Writings of the Late Hon'ble Mr. Justice M.G. Ranade, op. cit.*, p. 234.

4

ECONOMIC IDEAS

In 19th century India, economic ideas, analysis and theory were not of mere academic or intellectual interest. They were the very stuff of contemporary politics and journalism. The hegemonic aspects of colonial rule in India were based on two basic ideological notions: (a) that British rule was 'benevolent', that is, the British ruled India in the interests of the Indian people and they were developing and modernizing India; and (b) that British rule was invincible. The 19th century nationalist intelligentsia controverted the first of these notions in a fundamental manner, though they still accepted the second notion. Consequently, defence of colonialism or its basic critique became the chief form of ideological struggle between the alien rulers and the leaders and activists of the rising national movement. The latter had already by the first decade of the 20th century fully and scientifically worked out the main outlines of the nationalist critique of the economics of colonialism in India. The leaders of the later phases of the national movement were to rely heavily on this critique. They propagated it on a massive scale among the common people, but they made hardly any advance over it. Their politics were to be distinguished from the early moderate politics by greater political militancy and mass mobilization but not by the content of their economic critique of colonialism.

Justice Ranade's economic writings were a major weapon in this ideological struggle between colonialism and the nationalists. The consequence of this struggle was the gradual erosion of the British hegemony over the minds of the Indian people; it was to weaken and then destroy the halo of beneficence around British rule which had led the Indian people to acquiesce in this rule. It was inevitable that in time this erosion would spread to the political field and generate a popular anti-imperialist movement.

Ranade was a major member of the group of economists who subjected British colonialism in India to a basic economic critique and helped evolve an alternative path of economic development. He had, moreover, in G.V. Joshi an equally profound co-worker and in Gopal Krishna Gokhale a worthy disciple. Because of his deep learning and wide intellectual reach, extensive writing and speaking, multisided activity which covered almost every area of life from economics and politics to social and religious reform and re-writing of Indian history, and his high moral authority as a nationalist leader and social reformer, Ranade influenced the social, economic and political thinking of several generations of the Indians. In the economic field, Ranade covered almost every area, knitting industry, agriculture, finance, foreign trade, currency, tariff, role of the state, and economic theory into a single whole. He thus became the founding father of what came to be known as "Indian Political Economy".[1]

Ranade did not of course make a direct connection between the economic problem and politics. Not that he was unaware of the connection, but he believed that in the then stage of India's social development the economic problem was more important than the political problem.

From his college days, Ranade took an active interest in economics as a subject. Economics was one of the subjects he taught at Elphinstone College, Bombay, where he began his working life. His study of earlier and contemporary leading economists was extensive. Adam Smith, Ricardo, James Mill, John Stuart Mill, Malthus, Bastiat, McCulloch, Torren, Jevons and senior among British economists, Hamilton, Carey among the Americans, Fredrick List among the Germans, were some of the economists whose works he studied critically and mastered. He devoured blue books and government reports. His mastery of contemporary statistics was unmatched. In fact, he initiated the tradition among Indian nationalist economists of trying to acquire mastery of empirical data. The memoranda, petitions he prepared and the articles he wrote were based on unimpeachable data. Nobody was ever able to find a factual or statistical flaw in them. Whenever a young man came to him wanting his guidance in working in the cause of the nation, he would ask him to go through a blue book and prepare its digest. Only those who passed this test were taken under his wings.

As a student of history and of world economy, Ranade analysed Indian economy in a historical and comparative perspective; and he constantly tried to correlate Indian economic problems to the historical experience of other countries and to contemporary economic theories. As a wide-ranging thinker he also placed them in their social and political setting.

As the case of other nationalist economists, the backdrop to Ranade's economic thinking was provided by two fundamental problems. One was India's deteriorating economic condition and the phenomenal and growing poverty of the Indian masses. The other problem was that of the basically unbalanced, dependent and colonial structure of the economy. Referring to the unbalanced economic structure, Ranade wrote in 1890:

> "There can be no doubt that, whatever may have been our improvement in other respects, we have in recent times become more than ever dependent upon the single resource of Agriculture, precarious and contingent as that resource is, upon influences we cannot control or count upon with certainty. The coordination of industries, which regulates the due proportion of men who plough the soil and raise raw produce, with those who manufacture the raw produce and others still who exchange and distribute it, and the interplay of whose three-fold activities make a Nation thrive, was never a strong factor in our collective Social Polity. We have been all along like most Ancient Nations, more or less exclusively agricultural. But our contact with the world outside, and the freedom of Exchange which has resulted in consequence, have produced one most undesirable result. They have aggravated the situation by making us more than ever dependent upon a single and precarious resource. The Industry and Commerce of the Country, such as it was, is passing out of our hands and, except in the large Presidency Towns, the Country is fed, clothed,

> warmed, washed, lighted, helped and comforted generally, by a thousand Arts and Industries in the manipulation of which its Sons have everyday a decreasing share. Foreign Competition, not because it is foreign, but because it is the competition of Nature's powers against man's Labour, is the competition of organised Skill and Science against Ignorance and Idleness, is transforming the monopoly not only of wealth, but what is more important of skill, talent and activity to others."[2]

The balance between the agricultural and industrial sectors of the economy had been disrupted "to a greater extent than it was before". This had led to increasing ruralization—"a distinctly retrograde move"—and forced millions of artisans to fall back upon "the single and precarious resource of agriculture".

Another consequence, said Ranade, was that the country's economic life came more and more under foreign economic domination. Indian market was dominated by foreign manufactures. In addition, "our shipping is not ours, not even the coastal trade is carried on in our bottoms"; "our Banking is not ours, though to a large extent we find the money which finances the Exchange Banks"; "the Insurance and the Freight and the Commission Business are all Foreign Monopolies, and the Foreign Merchant's hand is seen trafficking direct with our producers in the remotest and smallest villages"; "the Railways are admittedly foreign Monopolies". Thus, pointed out Ranade, "political ascendancy is not the only particular vantage ground which we have lost. Commercial and manufacturing predominance naturally transfers political ascendancy, and in this our collapse has been even far more complete". Moreover, even though foreign political domination attracted "more attention", the "unfelt", the more invisible foreign domination was more "formidable" and "invidious" because it "paralyzes the springs of all the varied activities together making up the life of a nation".[3]

Increasingly, noted Ranade, the Indian economy bore a colonial character. It became a producer of raw materials and consumer of foreign manufactures. Earlier North America and British colonies had performed this function for England or the American War of

Independence and the granting of political autonomy to other colonies. India had, in the 19th century, taken the place of the old colonies and come to be regarded by its rulers "as a Plantation, growing raw produce to be shipped by British Agents in British Ships, to be worked into by British skill and capital, and to be re-exported to the Dependency by British merchants to their corresponding British Firms in India and elsewhere".[4]

Overall the sources of India's national income were being narrowed down and the Indian economy was, consequently, in a precarious condition: "When the whole situation is thus taken in at a view, we feel that we are standing on the edge of a precipice, and the slightest push down will drive us into the abyss below of unmixed and absolute helplessness."[5]

Ranade's three major concerns in the economic field were: Industrial development, agrarian structure and agricultural development and political economy. Like other nationalists, he gave intense and undivided commitment to economic development which he saw, above all, as the development of modern industry. He repeatedly pointed to the paralysis of the traditional handicraft industries under British rule. But he also accepted that their revival was no longer possible. "No Hand-made Industry", he wrote, "can hope to thrive in competition with industry moved by cheap natural Agents." The remedy of the existing backward and disrupted economic condition, therefore, lay in modern industrial development, which Ranade advocated with passion and urgency. The urgent task was to organize "cooperation" as the Indian capitalists had started doing and thus "to compete with the Foreigner" by working up raw materials through modern machines and thus, simultaneously, providing employment to India's working classes. True, this would mean working "against great odds", for Indians had to go against old traditions and to compete with advanced countries "whose industrial organization has been completed under more favourable circumstances than our own". And so he made one of his rare, fervent exhortations to his fellow countrymen:

> "This is the practical work which Providence has set down for us to learn under the best of teachers.... We have to improve

our Raw Materials, or import them when our soil is unsuited to their production. We have to organize Labour and Capital by co-operation and import freely Foreign Skill and Machinery, till we learn our lessons properly and need no help. We have rusticated too long; we have now to turn our apt hands to new work, and bend our muscles to sturdier and honester labour. This is the Civic Virtue we have to learn, and according as we learn it or spurn it we shall win or lose in the contest.... I feel sure it will soon become the creed of the whole Nation and ensure the permanent triumph of the modern spirit in this Ancient Land."[6]

From this point of view, citing Fredrick List, Ranade pointed out the difference between economic development and economic growth measured only in terms of increase in national income. "National well-being", he wrote, "does not consist only in the creation of the highest quantity of wealth measured in exchange value, independent of all variety of quality in that wealth, but in the full and many-sided development of all productive powers."

Moreover, wrote Ranade, in view of the fact that most of the arable land had been brought under cultivation and there was not much scope left for extended cultivation, industries were the only source left through which the pressure of population on land could be eased, and the physical needs of the increasing population met.

In any case, it was necessary to put an end to India's further ruralization and its exclusive dependence on agriculture, as it was, because of uncertain rainfall, a precarious source of livelihood. Dependence on agriculture had another negative feature—it was "under the bane of the Law of Diminishing Returns", while modern industries were not subject to any such law. It had also led to the absorption of waste lands and the exhaustion of soil through over-cultivation.

Modern industries had also a vital bearing "on the education of the intelligence and skill and enterprize of the Nation". A purely agricultural country represented a lower stage of civilisation. There was, in it, "a tendency to stagnation and absence of enterprize and the retention of antiquated prejudices." The increasing ruralization of India had meant "its rustication, i.e., a loss of power, and intelligence, and self-dependence". On the other hand, factories and mills could "far more effectively than Schools and Colleges give a new birth to the activities of the Nation".

Industrialization and the consequent urbanization were also necessary for healthy agriculture. Thriving towns and cities would provide the non-agricultural market divorced from which "no agriculture can be really productive". Moreover, industrialization was the only means through which the population pressure on land could be reduced. This emphasis on industry did not mean that agriculture was to be neglected. Ranade repeatedly stressed a proper coordination of the three forms of economic activity—agriculture, industry and trade. In fact, more than half of his economic writing and memorials pertained to agriculture.

Ranade rejected the theory of international trade with its emphasis on international division of labour according to which the natural role of India as a tropical country was to produce raw materials, while the European countries were suited to trade and industry. On the other hand, he held that India was fully capable of becoming a major industrial country. For proof, he pointed to the past achievements of India in handicraft manufactures, the wide production of raw materials needed by modern industries, the "natural aptitudes" of Indians for trade and industry and the "undeveloped but unlimited resources", and the existence of "peace and order".

The need was to strive hard and remove the man-made obstacles from the path. In this context, Ranade noted with enthusiasm the beginnings of modern industry in India. He was optimistic that, despite India's struggle for implanting modern industry being "of a very unequal character, a struggle between a Giant and a Dwarf," it was now "gathering up its forces, and marshalling them in order to ward off the evil effects of the first surrender that it had to make by way of homage to British skill capital and enterprise". Already, he wrote in 1893, Indians had in the last 40 years, invested nearly 500 million rupees in manufacturing, plantation, and mining industries. "This is an humble beginning, but it is a very hopeful one", he said. Another ground for satisfaction, however "slight and scarcely perceptible", was the increase of towns and slight increase in the relative proportions of urban and rural populations—in the Bombay Presidency the share of urban population having increased from 17 to 19 per cent from 1872 to 1891. Similarly, even though India still in the main exported raw materials and imported manufactures, change was noticeable even here. Exports of manufactured and partly manufactured goods were growing at a faster rate than the export of raw materials, and imports of raw materials were growing faster than the imports of manufactured goods.

Giving overt expression to his optimism and concluding his 1893 paper on the "Present State of Indian Manufactures and Outlook of the Same", Ranade said that despite having to work against "great odds"—old traditions, poverty of developed sources, "the hostile competition of advanced races, whose industrial organization has been completed under more favourable conditions than our own", and the Free-Trade policy of the Government—"we may win, if we will only persevere in our efforts, and direct them by cooperation on a large scale into proper channels".[7]

Apart from colonial domination, "the hostile competition of advanced races" and the free-trade policy of the Government, there were certain other obstacles to industrial development. The shortage of capital available for investment was one of these or obstacles: "Just as the Land in India thirsts for water, so the industry is parched up for want of capital". Why was this so? The accumulated capital, and savings of the Indian people were scanty, said Ranade. Moreover, a large part of this potential capital was mopped up by the state through taxation. In any case, the desire for accumulation was rather weak because of the absence of peace and security in the past and the religious ideals of life which condemned the "ardent pursuit of wealth". There was also "an almost complete absence of a landed gentry or wealthy middle class" which, in Ranade's calculation, were the chief agents of accumulation of capital and its use in agriculture, trade and industry. Then there was "the economic drain of wealth and talents" because of foreign domination.

Even so, Ranade believed, there was plenty of capital "ready to hand awaiting secure investment". The problem was that of its mobilization and utilization. Unfortunately, most of this capital was scattered and immobile. Indian social institutions and laws encouraged "subdivision and not concentration of wealth". The habit of mobilizing the scattered capital resources of the country through joint-stock companies was not developed. Instead, savings were either spent unproductively, for example, in purchase of expensive jewellery, or hoarded and buried under one form or another. For example, often they were invested in Government securities and post office banks and were, therefore, not available for productive investment. India also lacked modern banks and other credit institutions through which scattered savings could be canalized into modern industries. "Hoards of capital" were, of course, "stored up" in the Presidency and other Exchange banks; but they were not available to Indian entrepreneurs.

The remedy, said Ranade, lay in the people taking out their hoardings and turning them to "capital account", and in better organization of capital through the promotion of modern banks, insurance companies, etc., so that those who saved could be brought "face to face" with those who needed capital for investment. Above all, since modern industry made "large investments of capital a necessity, and thus handicaps all individual efforts beyond rivalry", Indians must learn to cooperate and combine individual efforts by adopting institution of joint-stock companies for large undertakings. In this respect, Ranade also pleaded for active state aid and encouragement.

The dearth of trained technical personnel was another factor hampering the growth of modern industry. The answer, said Ranade, lay in importing foreign technicians and training Indians in technical institutes in India and abroad and through "the far more practical discipline of Factories and Mills at work." In 1881, through the Poona Sarvajanik Sabha, Ranade appealed to the princes, big *zamindars*, the rich millionares of Bombay, and other rich Indians to endow scholarships to enable Indian students to go to England, France, Germany, Russia and the United States of America to study their arts and manufacture so that on their return they could help revive Indian economy and society. Citing the example of Japan and China in this respect, he pointed out that strong efforts to start cotton mills here and there could not compensate for the ongoing industrial prostration, for "the mechanical and engineering departments" of these mills were "entirely dependent upon imported skill for their very existence". Modern factories could "never be said to have taken root in the soil till we have a race of men among ourselves fully trained to plan, establish and work every department of manufacturing and trading with efficiency and cheap native skill", concluded the Sarvajanik Sabha appeal.[8]

According to Ranade, there was a positive correlation between industrial and economic development and a people's social institutions, custom, psychological make up—habits of mind—and culture in general. Change from a rural to an industrial economy presupposed, wrote Ranade, "a change of habits; it postulates the previous growth of culture and a spirit of enterprize, an alertness of mind, an elasticity of temper, a readiness to meet and conquer opposition, a facility of organization, social ambition and aspiration, a mobile and restless condition of capital and labour." All these bourgeois virtues developed over "centuries of Freedom and Progress". But if Indians wanted to develop into a manufacturing country they had to be acquired. Similarly, referring to the paucity of iron and coal in India, Ranade said that, though abundance of iron and coal explained the success of foreign competition, far more important than these materials was "the spirit and skill which work them and which conquered India long before Steam Power came into use". "If we but acquire the spirit and the skill", he exhorted, "the resources will be discovered in yet unexplored situations all over the country".

This weakness of the entrepreneurial spirit was, however, believed Ranade, not due to any inherent weakness of national spirit. He blamed Indian social institutions and laws, the past political condition, the prevailing religious ideals of life and in general conservative habits of mind for the absence of this spirit. Through his historical essays, he tried to show how this 'spirit', the qualities of daring and organization, a restless condition of mind, and the facility of organization were to be found in abundance in the days of Shivaji and his successors and how Brahmanical domination, under the Peshwas had led to retrogression.[9] The remedy to the present situation lay in the radical altering of the social, institutions and social outlook of the people and the imbibing of the new spirit of capitalism. "You cannot have a good economic system when your social arrangements are imperfect"[10]; and in his inaugural address at the Allahabad session of the Social Conference in 1892 he put his conception of the changes in the outlook and ideas and social practices in the form of a catechism: "A change from constraint to freedom, from credulity to faith, from status to contract, from authority to reason, from unorganized to organized life, from bigotry to toleration, from blind fatalism to a sense of human dignity".[11]

Ranade was a most consistent and vocal supporter of the idea that the state in India had to play a crucial role in the promotion of industrialization and economic development. He delineated, the active role of the state in the economy not only forcefully but even with some originality. Ranade was convinced that the Indian capitalist class on its own would find it difficult to industrialize the country for it lacked knowledge, had a weak financial base and faced a narrow internal market and uncertain business prospects. It would, on the other hand, respond positively if state support and protection were extended to it, and if it was covered against early risks of enterprise. Hence he advocated a comprehensive and systematic policy of state aid to individual enterprise. The other side of the model was that the state in an underdeveloped country had a duty, an obligation to actively aid economic development. "The state," he said, "is now more and more recognised as the National Organ for taking care of National needs in all matters in which individual and cooperative efforts are not likely to be so effective and economic as National effort. This is the correct view to take the true functions of the state."

State aid and encouragement to industry and agriculture could take many varied forms. Following were some of the ways, advocated by Ranade, for the promotion of economic development by the state:

(i) Since according to Ranade a major lacuna in Indian industrial effort was the lack of adequate and cheap capital in the hands of Indian entrepreneurs, state aid's most important role was "to supply this want". This it could do, first, by helping mobilize and concentrate the existing scattered capital and transform it into industrial capital through state assisted banks and other credit institutions which should be given facilities for the recovery of loans. The government should also help an industrial company to float its own debentures. Second, and more important, it should directly advance loans to Indian capitalists at low rates of interest and under proper supervision. The government might itself borrow money to make these loans, or it might create special financial corporations which would borrow funds from the Government at low interest and advance them as loans to the rural or urban industrialists. Local or municipal boards might also be empowered to perform this function of acting as intermediaries between the Government and the entrepreneurs. Government could lend the savings deposited with it, which were "wholly unproductive", to the local bodies, financial corporations and district corporate banks for this purpose. Thus, "each District might thus have a fund to develop its own way, and several Districts might combine together to support a strong undertaking for common advantage." The Government should, of course, exercise proper supervision over the disbursement of these loans: "with judicious supervision the whole face of the Country might be changed in the course of a few years."

(ii) The government should induce investment in new industries by providing security to the investors by giving guarantees of minimum profit similar to those given to railway companies. This guarantee was particularly needed for an industry like the iron and steel industry where "no dividend can be expected for the first few experimental years", and where "no capitalist would venture, unless the concessions are liberal, and a subsidy promised on the plan which helped the Guaranteed Railway Companies to obtain their capital." The other example held up for emulation by Ranade was that of the Culture System in Indonesia, though he grossly misunderstood the character and economic impact of the Culture System; that however, hardly mattered in his scheme of things, for the only lesson he wanted to draw was that of state support to industrial effort (Article no. 17). He also advocated, though with lesser emphasis, the grant of state subsidies to new industries "till private enterprise could support itself." At the same time, he conceded that the Government should reserve the right to share in the profits of the aided enterprises.

(iii) The government purchased a large part of stores abroad. These stores constituted a considerable part of Indian imports of manufactured goods. They included such items as equipment for the Indian army and police, materials for water, gas and sewage systems, hospital equipment and medical stores, iron, steel and cement and other materials required for docks, bridges, buildings and roads, telegraph and telephone equipment, stationery and other materials consumed by the administration, and tracks, bridges, rolling stock and building materials for state railways. All but an insignificant part of these stores were purchased in Britain. *Ranade* argued that the government should purchase these stores in India and thus give a powerful impetus to indigenous industrial efforts. Advocating a radical departure from the policy of *laissez faire,* he suggested that if some items of these stores are not available in India, the government should manufacture them in state factories. Generalizing this suggestion, he also asked the government, though in a rather low key, to pioneer new industries.

(iv) The government should collect and disseminate industrial and commercial information. It should also promote technical education in various ways. And to perform all these functions, it was necessary to set up a separate department of commerce and industries.

Even though emphasizing active state assistance, all his life Ranade held that finally, economic regeneration must come from Indian people's own efforts; self-help and self-reliance had to be their watchwords. This was the conclusion to his public lectures in 1872; and in his inaugural address to the first Industrial Conference in 1890, he said: "State help is, after all, a subordinate factor in the problem. Our own exertion and our resolution must conquer the difficulties, which are chiefly creation." And he exhorted Indians: "We have to work with a will, to pull long, and pull all, and to pull till we succeed."

In pursuance of this self-help, Ranade undertook or advocated several steps. He pioneered the Industrial Association of Western India in 1890 and the Industrial Conference which first met at Poona—in the same year with a view to promoting the creed of industrialism, awaken interest in industrial development, arouse the spirit of enterprise, create a confident and hopeful industrial outlook, and diffuse information regarding the scope and opportunities for various enterprises. His numerous articles and addresses on economic problems had the same objectives in view. He played an important part in the organization of several industrial ventures at Poona—the Cotton and Silk Spinning and Weaving Factory, the Metal Manufacturing Factory, the Poona Mercantile Bank, the Poona Dyeing Company, and the Reay Paper Mill.[12] According to Gopal Krishna Gokhale, "most of the industrial and commercial undertakings that have sprung up in Poona during the last twenty years owe a great deal to his inspiration, advice, or assistance."[13]

Surprisingly, except in the early 1870s, Ranade had little to say on Swadeshi. In his 1872 public lectures at Poona, he popularized the idea of *Swadeshi*, of preferring Indian goods, even if they were costlier or inferior to foreign goods. These lectures so inspired the listeners that several of them, including, Ganesh Vasudeo Joshi, popularly known as Sarvajanik Kaka and Vasudeo Phadke, who later led an armed foray against the government, took a vow to wear and use only *Swadeshi* articles.[14] Earlier in Poona, just after coming there, Ranade and Joshi had started a cooperative company to deal in *Swadeshi* goods. In 1874 he joined Joshi in organizing on behalf of the Poona Sarvajanik Sabha the first annual exhibition of *Swadeshi* articles, produced in the small-scale factories of Maharashtra. But not a word on the subject is to be found in his later writings and addresses. Perhaps, as brought out below, what he said about the drain and tariff protection of not making 'vain efforts' also explains his later attitude to *Swadeshi*.

The agrarian problem occupied a large part of Ranade's intellectual activity. He dealt at length with the relation between the peasant and the colonial state, the peasant and the landlord, and agriculture and industry. He also put forward the broad outlines of a capitalist agrarian structure as an alternative to the existing semi-feudal agrarian structure. In fact, all his analysis was based on the need for 'free' peasants and investing landlords.

Ranade advocated that agrarian relations should be based on the creation of two new and basic agrarian classes which would live side by side: (a) a large petty land-owning peasantry, which would be free of all encumberances, whether of the state or the landlords, and which would be bolstered by a permanent and low land tax and the provision of cheap credit through agricultural banks; and (b) a large class of capitalist farmers and landlords who, being unhampered by any tenancy rights or other restrictions, would be in complete possession of their land and in a position to invest capital, improve the soil, use fertilisers and better seeds, and utilise the latest, advanced techniques.

In this respect he stood for approval and imitation of the pattern of landownership, based on the growth of absolute property, both in the landlord class and in the peasantry, which had been brought into existence in Prussia by the middle 19th century. In Prussia in 1860, he pointed out, 15 per cent of cultivable land belonged to the state or the church, 44 per cent to large estate owners, 35 per cent to peasant proprietors, and 5 per cent to petty owners. Thus, he approvingly remarked that the land had been divided equally between "the rich landlords and the poor Free men", and the feudal serf converted into a free proprietor and the feudal lord into an unencumbered owner of his property. Applying the lessons of Prussia to India, Ranade advised: "High and petty farming, with an upper ten thousand of the holders of large landed estates, and a vast mass of peasant farmers, this mixed constitution of rural society is necessary to secure the stability and progress of the country." He also hoped that a proper class balance would be struck between the "upper ten thousand" and the "vast mass of peasant farmers", once the latter grow "in thrift, in knowledge and in power of combination."[15]

How these two new productive agrarian classes were to be brought into existence? Ranade had two sets of remedies to offer. In the *ryotwari* areas, the permanent settlement of land revenue at low rates would transform the depressed 'state tenants' into sturdy peasant-proprietors, who would be able to borrow from agricultural banks and moneylenders for making improvements in land. At the same time, in a regime of free competition and in the absence of any restrictions and encumberances on land, those among the moneyed classes who were willing and keen to perform the functions of capitalist landlords would buy the land of "the indifferent and lazy" *ryots*. He was also convinced that such a class of people who possessed "intelligence, wealth, thrifty habits, knowledge, and power of combination" did exist in India. On the other hand, the thrifty, hard-working *ryot* would slowly "extend his operations, and rise to a better position", i.e. become a capitalist farmer or what would be later called a *kulak*. Also, in course of time, he hoped, "the provident and thrifty classes will succeed to the ownership of land, and a class of landlords would spring up all over the country, whose interest will be to make the most of the resources of the soil, and of the great public works constructed by the government. It was because of the fear that restrictions on peasant's right to alienate or transfer land with a view to saving him from expropriation by the moneylender would check the inevitable tendency towards "concentration of the landed capital of the country" in the hands of the more efficient and resourceful peasants and capitalists that Ranade opposed all such restrictions and argued for free transferability of land.

Ranade worked out elements of the concept of Indian Political Economy in several of his articles, but it took concrete and well-worked out form in his classic address on "Indian Political Economy" delivered at the Deccan College, Poona in 1892 (Article no. 19). His basic formulations have been discussed at length by several economists. Their influence was felt by most of Indian economic writers till the 1930s, and even till the 1940s, when the influence first of Alfred Marshall and the Neo-Classicists and then Keynes and Keynesians started becoming predominant. His formulations were also subscribed to on a wide scale by his contemporaries, and not only by economists like G.V. Joshi and G. Subramaniya Iyer but also others who commented on economic issues in the Press and on the platform. Just as in his economic policy formulations he had used the historical experience of other countries, in his theoretical framework he was deeply influenced by 19th century economists. In particular, he turned to those European and American economists who were dissenting in important aspects from many of the tenets of British Classical Political Economy—Fredrick List, Adam Miller, Hamilton and Henry Carey. He was highly critical of the position of English Classical economists like Adam Smith, Ricardo, Senior,

Bastiat, James Mill, Torren, McCulloch, and Malthus, though he was influenced by John Stuart Mill and used him to support several of his own propositions.[16]

Ranade denied the claim, quite popular among Indian administrators, that the assumptions of classical political economy were universally and demonstrably true or valid for all times and places, and for all stages of economic development. These assumptions had been born out of specific conditions of England and they furnished "valid explanations" of the economic condition of only those societies of which they were "approximately true". But, in fact, they "do not absolutely hold good of even the most advanced societies;" and they had hardly any validity in a backward, stagnant agricultural country like India where not competition and contract but status and custom and tradition ruled. To quote him at length:

"It is obvious that in Societies like ours, they are chiefly conspicuous by their absence. With us an average individual man is, to large extent, the very antipodes of the Economical man. The family and the caste are more powerful than the individual in determining his position in life. Self-interest in the shape of desire of wealth is not absent, but it is not the only principal motor. The Pursuit of Wealth is not the only ideal aimed at. There is neither the desire nor the aptitude for free and unlimited competition except within certain predetermined grooves or groups. Custom and State Regulations are far more powerful than Competition, and Status more decisive influence than Contract. Neither Capital nor Labour is mobile, and enterprising and intelligent enough to shift from place to place. Wages and Profit are fixed, and not elastic and responsive to charge of circumstances. Population follows its own Law, being cut down by Disease and Famine, while production is almost stationary, the bumper harvest of one year being needed to provide against uncertainties of alternate bad seasons. In a society so constituted, the tendencies assumed as axiomatic, are not only not operative but are actually deflected from their proper direction. You might as well talk of the tendency of mountains to be washed away into the sea, or of the valleys to fill up, or of the Sun to get cold, as reasons for our practical conduct within a measurable distance of time.[17]

Second, Ranade gave numerous instances to show that the past practice of British statesmen and the contemporary practice of other nations did not at all conform to the precepts or assumptions of Classical economics. He wrote, "this conflict of practice with theory not in one, but all points, not in one place or country, but all over the world, distinguishes contemporary History." He also pointed out in another context, that Indian problems and conditions were "widely divergent" from those in Britain and were closer to those in Continental Europe and, therefore, "the lessons to be derived from the study of Continental Economy have a more practical bearing than the maxims contained in the usual textbooks of English Political Economy." Even in India, Ranade said, the British did not strictly adhere to these precepts in giving guarantees to railways and help to plantation industries or in trying to preserve through legislation petit culture by tenants. At the same, he remarked sarcastically, "the absolute Truths of Political Economy, however, are appealed to as a justification for a curious change of front. Men who come from a country where private property in land is most absolute, develop on their arrival here a taste for Socialistic Doctrines."

Third, Ranade pointed out that the scientific claims of Classical economics had been seriously questioned by European and American economists and thinkers such as Hamilton, Carey, August Comte, Sismondi, Gioga, Ludovico, Muller and List, and were under attack even by several English thinkers and economists such as Cairns, Bagehot, Sidgwick, Cliffe Leslie, Jevsons, Laing, and Maxwell Melvill. Moreover, some of the Classical economists themselves, for example, John Stuart Mill, and even Adam Smith had been at pains to avoid making claims of absoluteness and universality for their science.

Fourth, Classical economics, might at the most, explain static economic conditions of a society but could hardly cope with the process of dynamic economic development.

Keeping all these factors in view, the conclusion was inescapable, said Ranade; that the principles or laws of economics were not abstract and universal like those of physics or astronomy but relative and historically conditioned and derived; they differed in time and space. Hence, the specific stage of economic development of a people and not abstract economic theories should be the decisive factor in determining economic policies for a country.

We may summarise Ranade's general economic thought in the form of four broad formulations: (i) the same propositions of economics or economic doctrines cannot be applied to countries at different stages of economic development; (ii) these propositions should be formulated in the context of the general social conditions and economic needs of the country; (iii) economic ideas and policies should serve and be subjected to socially derived and socially integrated goals and perspectives; and (iv) since India's economic conditions and interest differed from England's, the principles of economics applicable to it must also be different or at least should be differently applied. All these formulations have been very significant in the development of economic thinking and policy perspectives in India. Certainly, hardly any economist or political leader has questioned them. At the same time, it would not be correct to suggest, as some have, that Ranade initiated any specifically 'Indian economics' or 'Indian system of economic ideas or theories'. Ranade did not discover or put forward any new economic laws which would be specifically applicable to Indian conditions. His economic thought was really an effort to adjust the assumptions and theories of the Classical economists and their later-day European, American and British critics to the Indian economic reality. It might almost be said that the 'Indian Political Economy' which Ranade tried to bring into being and which got the support of his contemporaries as well as the next two generations of economists in India, was more an attitude of mind, an approach towards Indian economic problems, and a method of economic reasoning than a system of economic thought.

REFERENCES

1. Chandra, Bipin, *Ranade's Economic Writings* (New Delhi: Gian Publishing House), 1990, p. XIV.

2. Chandra, Bipin, *The Rise and Growth of Economic Nationalism in Modern India* (New Delhi: People's Publishing House), 1966.
3. *Ibid.*, p. 410.
4. *Ibid.*, p. 411.
5. *Ibid.*, p. 272.
6. *Ibid.*, p. 425.
7. *Ibid.*, p. 426.
8. Paravate, T. V., *Mahadev Gobind Ranade* (Bombay: Asia Publishing House), 1963, pp. 280-287.
9. Ranade, Ramabai, *Miscellaneous Writings of the Late Hon'ble Mr. Justice M.G. Ranade, op. cit.*, p. 231.
10. *Ibid.*
11. *Ibid.*, pp. 116-17.
12. Mankar, G. A., *A Sketch of the Life and Works of the Late Mr. Justice M.G. Ranade* (Bombay: Dayabhai), 1902, Vol. I.
13. *Speeches and Writings of Gopal Krishan Gokhale* (Bombay: Asia Publishing House), 1962, p. 927.
14. Paravate, T. V., *Mahadev Gobind Ranade, op. cit.*, pp. 77-78.
15. Chandra, Bipin, *Ranade's Economic Writings, op. cit.*, p. XLVI.
16. *Ibid.*, p. 100.
17. *Ibid.*, p. 101.

5

ON SOCIAL REFORMS

Contact with Western life and thought introduced into India a new heaven. As it gradually spread, the minds of sundry men here and there throughout India became in greater or less degree illumined with a new sense of values, and became uncomfortable in the face of social customs which that new sense of values condemned. These customs were child-marriage, enforced widowhood, ill-assorted marriages (i.e. between old men and young girls), the dowry-system with its accompanying evils and hardships, extravagant expenditure on marriage festivities, the seclusion of women and the withholding of education from them, the regarding of foreign travel as sinful, the caste-system with its breaking up of the social body into a number of exclusive parts which will not intermarry and will not dine with one another, the holding of a large proportion of the population as outcastes or pariahs whose touch is defiling, customs of obscenity connected with the Holi and other festivals, and the profession of the nautchgirl. From his college days Ranade had been among those social reformers, i.e. who realised that these customs were evils which weakened and poisoned the life of the people, and who sought to find and apply the right remedies. Ranade was an ardent social reformer, and in the period of his life with which we are now dealing, he did yeoman service for the cause.

In 1884, B.M. Malabari, the renowned Bombay poet, journalist, and social reformer, wrote two pamphlets—one on "Child-Marriage" and the other on "Compulsory Widowhood". These are known as *Malabari Notes.* They were sent to all the official and the non-official leaders in India, and also to England. They gave a great impetus to the attack upon two of the most glaring of India's social evils, and marked the beginning of a period of hot agitation and bitter discussion, which lasted till 1891. Ranade had promised Malabari that he would help him in every way in his crusade, and loyally he kept his promise. His general opinion on the matter is indicated in the following paragraph:

> "After making all allowances, it cannot be denied that Hindu society contrasts very unfavourably with all other civilised races in both the points noticed so prominently by Mr. Malabari. It is also not denied that early marriage leads to early consummation, and thence to the physical deterioration of the race, that it sits as a heavy weight on our rising generation, enchains their aspirations, denies them the romance and freedom of youth, cools their love of study, checks enterprise, and generally dwarfs their growth, and fills the country with pauperism, bred of over-population by weaklings and sickly people, and lastly that it leads in many cases to all the horrors of early widowhood."[1]

Malabari's proposals involved getting government to pass a law laying down the minimum age at which girls might be married, and in other ways legislating on matters concerning Hindu marriage. The orthodox party were horrified at the idea of making such a request to government, for it seemed to them wrong and irreligious. State action was also opposed by many men whose real social reform was beyond all questions—they included Dr. R.G. Bhandarkar and Sir Narayan Chandawarkar—their position being that so long as popular sentiment on the subject remained unchanged, State action, whether legislative or executive, would not only be important to secure the object in view, but would not unlikely prove harmful to the cause of real reform by provoking hostile forces which were at the time inactive and dormant. Ranade however vigorously supported the proposal to seek for a remedy through legislative enactment.

The Government of India sent *Malabari Notes* down to the Provincial Governments and to the leaders of thought and opinion with a request that it should be informed of their views. This fanned the interest in the controversy. There were meetings and counter meetings, petitions and counter-petitions.

In this personal reply to Government's request for his views on *Malabari Notes,* Ranade said that in the absence of a self-regulating power in Hindu Society, "the only way to secure the emancipation of the Hindu community from this bondage to past ideas is to withdraw one by one these fetters of so-called religious injunctions, and turn them into civil restraints, which are more amenable to change and adaptation."[2] He proposed State action on the following lines :

(a) That minimum marriageable age-limits both for boys and girls should be fixed by law, not compulsory in the sense of annulling marriages contracted before attaining the said limits, but only permissive in the sense of leaving the parties concerned freedom to question the binding character of the marriage so contracted—the age limit to be 16 to 18 for boys, and 10 to 12 for girls, subject to exceptions in particular castes localities.

(b) That Municipal and Local Boards should be empowered to certify ages and that the parties concerned should be required to obtain licences from these Boards, before marriages were solemnised.

(c) That the Universities should, after reasonable notice, confine their honours and distinctions, to those who, in addition to their other qualifications submit to the condition of remaining single during their College or School course.

(d) That the Penal Code be amended so far as to declare sexual intercourse with a girl under 14 to be rape.

(e) That men of 45 and upward should be prohibited by law from marrying young virgins; so also the marriage of young men with girls older than themselves should he prohibited as being unnatural and mischievous.

(f) That a second marriage during the lifetime of the first wife should be allowed only if there be in the first wife one of the defects in view of which the *Sastras* sanctioned such a marriage.

When the Government of India examined the replies to its inquiry regarding opinion on *Malabari Notes,* it found that there was a majority against the reform proposals, and accordingly it decided to make no move in the matter. In promulgating its decision it said that "interference by the State is undesirable, and that the reforms advocated by Mr. Malabari, which affect the social customs of many races with probably as many points of differences as of agreement, must be left to the improving influences of time, and to the gradual operation of the mental and moral development of the people by the spread of education."[3] The reformers were of course deeply disappointed. Ranade faced the situation with his usual calm optimism. He saw considerable gain in the prolonged agitations and acute discussions that had awakened the public mind on the question.

In 1884, with the onset of the social reform movement, a particular case focused on an evil practice, which became a centre of hot controversy. This was a suit filed by one Dadaji for the handing over to him of the girl Rakhmabai, to whom he had been married when she was 13, and he was 20. Rakhmabai was the daughter of one Mr. Pandurang, who died in 1867, worth 25,000 rupees. His wife afterwards married again, and therefore according to Hindu law forfeited her right to her late husband's income, which passed to his daughter. When Rakhmabai became mature, Dadaji asked that she be sent to his house, but agreed to postponement owing to her being still young. In 1884, however, he was determined to get her to his home and had thus applied to the court. The reason which Rakhmabai pleaded for not going to her husband's house was that he was consumptive, illiterate, and uncultured. The lower court decided in her favour, but the higher court decided against her, decreeing that she must go to live with her husband or, if she refused, must be punished with imprisonment. The whole matter showed what the position of a woman in Hinduism was—for a woman married in childhood could be compelled to go and live with a husband who was not only unequal but also repulsive to her. In 1887, Principal Wordsworth of the Elphinstone College, established a Rakhmabai Defence Committee, and among others Ranade took part in its chivalrous work.[4]

The burning passion with which Ranade felt the wrongs inflicted upon women by the social customs of Hinduism, is shown by an incident that happened in May of 1887, at a meeting of the *Oratory Encouragement Society*, when the subject of Woman's Rights was being discussed. Several of the speakers had, to the evident satisfaction of the audience, displayed a very reactive attitude towards women, pouring contempt upon the female character and talking of the dangers of revolutionary change in the ancient *Veda*-based Hindu Society. Ranade, speaking at the end in his capacity as the chairman of the meeting, passed over the other subjects and devoted two whole hours to the issue, 'woman's rights.' Speaking trenchantly and passionately, he said that an endeavour had been made to prove that the way to keep husband and wife together was by means of punishment and imprisonment, and that it was woman that was the blameable party. Both the reasoning and the charge were false. The Sastras show that in ancient days, women were always protected, served, and honoured by their men relatives. When we ascribe such faults to women, we are actually finding these faults in our mother, daughters, sisters, and wives, and it is astonishing that we do not see that no greater ingratitude can be imagined than to disgrace them thus. Ranade seems to have felt in the attitude of the speakers a sort of bravado, a cowardly valour shown at the expense of the defenceless women, and it made his blood boil. "We should feel ashamed", he cried, "that people all over the world, having advanced farther than we, are despising us—but leaving that aside, if the valour of our manhood is to be exercised against the women-folk of our homes, that is the lowest depth of baseness."[5]

Perhaps the greatest thing that Ranade did for social reform was his work in connection with the Indian National Social Conference. When the Indian National Congress was founded at Bombay, in 1885, the leaders felt that the national movement should not be exclusively political, but that side by side with the political questions, matters relating to the country's social economy should be considered. In accordance with this view, Dewan Bhadur R. Ragunath Rao and Ranade gave addresses on social reform at the meeting of the first Congress. However the leaders, after much careful thought, came to the conclusion that it would be better if the Congress did not make it part of its function to deal directly with the discussion of social questions. Those who felt keenly the urgency of the social problems resolved, after mature deliberation, to start a separate movement, to be called *The Indian National Social Conference.* Ragunath Rao and Ranade were the moving spirits, and the first Social Conference was held at Madras in December 1887. It was closely associated with the Congress, as it was followed up immediately and held in the same *mandap* (i.e. marquee). The position, as Ranade once put it, was as follows: "The Congress leaders have granted us permission to carry on in their camp our propaganda on our own responsibility."[6] The Congress and the Conference together made Indians feel that politically they were a united nation, and that their social arrangement were being subjected to the inspiring influences of the national spirit.

The object of the National Social Conference was to stimulate and to strengthen the forces of reform by bringing together every year, in mutual consultation, representatives of the various associations and movements which, scattered over all India, were struggling with the social evils. A great deal of good and hopeful work in the way of social reform was being done here and there, throughout the country. The Conference brought this work to limelight and made the inspiration and example of it available for others. It strengthened the hands of local societies, formulated methods, and guided the reforming aspirations. This unifying of the social movement in India was an achievement of great importance. It brought the ideas of social reform home to a much wider public, and it gave powerful reinforcement to the scattered reformers in their struggle with inertia and reaction. Ranade threw himself into the work with immense zeal and with untiring perseverance. The Social Conference Organisation was launched in 1898. Ragunath Rao was the Secretary, but Ranade was the guiding hand and the inspiring mind. They sent out letters in all directions, stirring people up to start social reform societies in different places. There was, of course, a strong local society in Poona, and through its agency, in 1889, the reform oaths were taken by 549 persons. The vows included abstinence from alcoholic drinks, cessation from the practice of dowries, agreement to widow re-marriage, promise to give education to girls and disagreement to child-marriages. People of high position who took part in the Poona society, included inamdars, jagirdars, and chiefs of the Deccan. The Maharajas of Baroda and Indore volunteered to find it. Mussalmans and Christians as well as Hindus joined the conference.

Each year when the Social Conference met in one of the provincial capitals of India, Ranade gave an address in which he summarised the reports that had come to him from Social Reform Associations from all over the country. The following is a typical opening to these addresses: "Mr. President and Gentlemen," he said at Allahabad, in 1892, "once more we meet in this busy week of December, this time in your historical and holy city, to take stock of our year's achievements, to count our losses and gains, and to pledge ourselves to help each other in the unceasing struggle to better our condition."[7]

Reading those Conference addresses one feels as if one were watching an able General directing a campaign. We see him keeping his eye always on the ultimate goal, and judging every apparent success or failure in its relation to that goal. We see him forging ahead, while being fully aware that impatience and over enthusiasm do not help in the long run. We see him keeping up the morale of his army by infusing into it his own robust and reasoned optimism.

In the Conference addresses Ranade who was at the centre of so much controversy, had to deal with many questions on social reform. For example, there was a question: What place should social reform take in patriotic activity? Many men of patriotic spirit were condemning the social reform propaganda as mischievous, or were regarding it with a sullen disapproval, or felt that it could very well wait until the political situation had been satisfactorily dealt with. To this last point of view even K.T. Telang, much to Ranade's distress, lent the weight of his great influence, when, in a famous speech, he advocated advancing along "the line of least distance".

Ranade's mind was essentially balanced and comprehensive. He saw human life as an organism and hated partial or extremist methods of improvement. The opinion which he held consistently all through his career and expressed again and again, was that it is impossible to separate politics and social reform. Perhaps, the most striking expression that he gave to this opinion was in the last year of his life when, as President of the First Bombay Provincial Social Conference, held at Satara, he urged that the different fields of human activity are inseparably interrelated, like the perfume cannot be seperated from the rose:

"Whether in the political, or social, or religious, or commercial, or manufacturing, or aesthetical spheres; in literature, in science, in art, in war, in peace; it is the individual and collective man who has to develop his powers by his own exertions in conquering the difficulties in his way. If he is down for the time, he has to get up with the whole of his strength, physical, moral, and intellectual, and you may as well suppose that he can develop one of those elements of strength and neglect the others, as try to separate the light from the heat of the sun or the beauty and fragrance from the rose. You cannot have a good social system when you find yourself low in the scale of political rights, nor can you find yourself low in the scale of political rights, nor can you be fit to exercise political rights and privileges unless your social system is based on reason and justice. You cannot have a good economical system when your social arrangements are imperfect. If your religious ideals are low and grovelling, you cannot succeed in social, economical or political spheres. This inter-dependence is not an accident, but is the law of our nature. Like the members of our body, you cannot have strength in the hands and the feet if your internal organs are in disorder; what applies to the human body holds good of the collective humanity we call the society or state. It is a mistaken view which divorces considerations political from social and economical, and no man can be said to realise his duty in one aspect who neglects his duties in the other directions."[8]

Though a keen member of the Prarthana Samaj, Ranade yet deprecated the view that it was only through a religious reformation that advance could be made, and that all the efforts of the reformers ought to be directed towards the purification of religion. Such a view was too one-sided for his conception of the organic nature of society and, moreover, he was always afraid of breaking the historical continuity and afraid of making the orthodox people reactionists out of a mere spirit of opposition.

Nevertheless, a close study of Ranade's social reform addresses leads us to say that he does really in his own way give religion the predominant place in his social philosophy, or at any rate he leaves that place empty for religion to occupy. We can trace clearly in his writings the recognition that religion is the central spring of life, and that in religion we touch the organic life-power which can flow out in healthy activity to all the members. For, in discussing measures for the reform of outward conditions, Ranade is constantly recurring to the importance of what we might call inward personal religion. In an address delivered at the Hislop College during the Nagpur Conference of 1891, he is reported as having said :

"Some there were who thought that when they were asked to lend their support to reform, there was some objective reality outside themselves that they had to deal with. There was no such thing. The thing to be reformed was their own self, heart and head and soul, their own prejudices were to be removed, their superstitions to be eradicated, their courage to be strengthened, their weaknesses to be conquered, in fact their character to be formed again so as to suit the times, so as to fit with the spirit of the age."[9]

At the Conference at Amraoti in 1897, Ranade argued that the root of India's troubles was the possession of the people's minds by a set of wrong ideas. He asks :

"Now what have been the inward forms or ideas which have been hastening our decline during the past three thousand years? These ideas may be briefly set forth as isolation, submission to outward force or power more than to the voice of the inward conscience, perception of fictitious differences between men and women, due to heredity and birth, passive acquiescence in evil or wrong-doing, and a general indifference to secular well-being, almost bordering upon fatalism. These have been the root ideas of our ancient social system. They have as their natural result led to the existing family arrangements where the woman is entirely subordinated to the man and the lower castes to the higher castes, to the length of depriving men of their natural respect for humanity."[10]

Ranade insists that the only way in which the evils of the time can be removed is by placing ourselves under the discipline of better ideas. "The current of these ideas must be changed, and in the place of the old worship we paid to them, we must accustom ourselves and others to worship and reverence to new ideals." He, therefore, seeks to inculcate the idea of a wide fraternity in place of proud isolation. He seeks also to show that heredity and birth are not the only factor determining a person's life for good or evil. "The Law of *Karma* can be controlled and set back by properly trained will, when it is made subservient to a higher will than ours ... Necessity or the Fates are faint obstacles in the way of our advancement if we devote ourselves to the law of Duty."

As an antidote to the poisonous idea that "all human life is vanity and dream, and we are not much concerned with it"—an idea which he characterises as "atheism in its worst form"—he puts forth "a healthy sense of the true dignity of our nature, of man's high destiny." But, above all, he insists on the need to get away from childish dependence upon authority:

"With too many of us, a thing is true or false, righteous or sinful, simply because somebody in the past has said that it is so. Duties and obligations are duties and obligations, not because we feel them to be so, but because somebody reputed to be wise has laid it down that they are so ... When we abandon ourselves entirely to this helpless dependence on other wills, it is no wonder that we become helpless as children in all departments of life."[11]

The new idea is not to be the idea of a rebellious overthrow of all authority, but that of freedom responsible to the voice of God in us. "Revere all human authority," Ranade says, "pay your respects to all Prophets and all revealations, but never let this reverence and respect come in the way of the dictates of conscience, the Divine command in us." It is this self-respect, or rather respect for the God in us, which Ranade singles out as requiring above all things to be cultivated. We see again and again in his writings the appreciation of the fact that victory for social reform is to be won not by mere modification of social institutions but by the changing of the hearts of individuals. His emphasis is on the inward aspect:

"Reforms in the matter of infant marriage and enforced widowhood, in the matter of temperance and purity, inter-marriage between castes, the elevation of the low castes, and the re-admission of converts, and the regulation of our endowments and charities, are reforms only so far and no further, as they check the influence of the old ideas, and promote the growth of the new tendencies." "The issue," he said, at Madras, in 1898, "is not this or that particular reform about which people have so much controversy, but the general spirit of purity, justice, equality, temperance, and mercy, which should be infused into our minds and which should illumine our hearts. Is it to be the spirit of justice, charity, mercy, toleration and appreciation of all, or is it to be exclusiveness, haughtiness, pride, cruelty and misery of all kinds ? The choice lies with us and we may choose which we prefer."[12]

The question of method in social reform is always important and often controversial, and Ranade frequently refers to it. Four main methods were advocated and used for effecting the desired reforms and for inducing people to support them. These were: (1) the traditional method, (2) the conscience method, (3) the legislation method, and (4) the rebellion method. Ranade made use of all these except the last. The method of rebellion meant separating from the conservative, orthodox people and forming a new camp. He recognised that this way with its sweeping aside of compromising and complicating bonds, had its merits, but he thought that its demerits ruled it out. For it broke the historic continuity and tended to make the orthodox reactionist out of the sheer spirit of opposition. "I am," he said, "constitutionally inclined to put more faith in the other methods."[13]

The traditional method seeks to temper the winds of reform to the sensitiveness of orthodoxy by showing that the reforms are not really innovations at all but are the carrying out of the spirit and even of the letter of the ancient scriptures. Ranade, always averse to breaking completely with the past and keen to carry the orthodox party with him if possible, made much of this method. Two contributions that he made to the literature of the subject are notable. The one was written about 1870 and was called *Vedic Authorities for Widow Marriage*. It is a fine example of the moral fervour, the discreet caution, and the studious research which Ranade showed in these controversies. He writes:

"The advocates of re-marriage have never maintained that a woman after her husband's death should not live a life of a single devotion to her deceased husband. They freely allow that such heroic self-sacrifice to a sentiment is peculiarly meritorious. But a woman who cannot live this species of life, a woman who is widowed when a girl, before she knew what her duties as a wife were—surely such woman cannot practise this devotion. It is on behalf of such women that this reform is a peremptory and crying want, and to require them to live a life of devotion in the manner. Manu prescribes a simple mockery of all religion and justice."

And his summing up of his examination of the sacred texts is:

"There is thus express permission in the Vedas, express permission in the Smriti law common to all the *yugas*, and express permission in the special law for the Kaliyuga; and it has been shown that all the prohibitory texts are mostly very vague and general, and so far from abrogating, only restrict the number of contingencies when remarriage is permitted by the law. And such of them as are more particular are controlled by the Parashara text, first because it is so special, and secondly, because it is the binding authority for the age."[14]

The other contribution was a paper which he wrote in 1888 for Dayaram Gidumal's book *The Status of Woman in India*. The paper was entitled "The Sastric Texts on the Subject of Infant Marriage," and in the following year it appeared in the *Sarvajanik Sabha Journal* with the title "The Sutra and Smriti Dicta on the Subject of Hindu Marriage." In that paper Ranade traces the deterioration of the status of woman in Hindu society, from the time represented in the *Sutra* writings when late marriage was the rule and widow remarriage was common, when monogamy held sway, when female education was approved, and woman's place in society was one of freedom and dignity, to the time when early and even infant marriage came to be insisted on in the name of religion, and the remarriage of widows condemned, and when so far as the male was concerned monogamy lost its strictness, when women were put on a level with *Sudras* in respect of exclusion from Vedic learning and performance of Vedic rites, and were condemned to life-long pupilage, first to the father, afterwards to the husband, and lastly to the son. He analyses the opinions of the *Smriti* writers and concludes that for girls 12 may be taken as the authoritative minimum age for marriage and 16 as the minimum age of consent (i.e., the age below which consummation of marriage is not permitted), while for boys the corresponding ages are 18 and 25 respectively:

"Leaving the old *Sutra* period as too remote to influence the present condition of our population, no such objection can be urged to the minimum limits laid down above 12 and 18, and 16 and 25, as supported by the vast majority of the really authoritative texts. Those who seek reform in this matter do not desire to turn marriage into an affair of mutual romantic love. They do not want to thrust aside the parental authority, or to diminish the sense of responsibility now felt. They advocate a return from modern corruptions to the real sense of the old *Smriti* texts... It is hoped that after the present reaction subsides, men will come to see that in clinging to the existing order of things they are really setting at nought the traditions of their own best days and the injunctions of their own *Sastras*, leaving aside all considerations of duty and expediency; and that, in calling for a change on the old lines, the reformers seek not to revolutionize, but only to lop off the diseased over-growth and excrescence and to restore vitality and energy to the social organism."[15]

As regards what we have called the conscience-method, which makes its appeal directly to the sense of right and wrong, Ranade constantly uses it. He reminds us that the voice of God is the only voice to which we are bound to listen, and tells us that "all of us cannot listen to it when we desire it, because from long neglect and dependence upon outside help, we have benumbed this faculty of conscience within us." In pursuance of this method, reformers strengthened themselves by taking pledges regarding female education, widow-remarriage, abstinence from alcoholic liquor, suppression of child-marriages, etc.

The legislation method meant the enforcement of reform, either through the agency of the caste authority or through the agency of the State. This method was, Ranade said, "a constraint imposed by the wise upon the ignorant in their common interest. It has its merits as well as demerits, but it must be advocated only in those cases in which the first two have no chance of success, for it is a coercive method, which should not be resorted to until other ways have been tried."[16]

The controversy that raged round what is known as the Age of Consent Bill is interesting not only as one of the landmarks in the agitation for social reform in India, but also because of the way in which it brought this method of reform by legislation into the full blaze of criticism and defence.

Ranade stood up stoutly for the policy of invoking the aid of the State to raise the age of consent from 10 to 12. There was, however, hot opposition to the proposal, not only from the right wing of religious orthodoxy, but also from many of the social reformers themselves, and particularly from the new school of thought that was coming to vigorous life under the leadership of B.G. Tilak. Tilak had come to the conclusion that the root necessity was political liberty, and that this end should be pursued to the exclusion, if necessary, of everything else and he felt that by all means the independence, confidence, and pride of nationality must be fostered among the Indians. He felt that the social reformers were too deeply tinctured with Western ideas, and that their criticism and denunciation of national institutions and national customs would lead to the disintegration of the nation. At first he was not altogether hostile, though he thought that the masses were not prepared for general legislation. He proposed that those who approved of the reforms should bind themselves to carry them out, and that the legislation should apply to the reformers alone and not the masses. A meeting was held to discuss his idea, but it did not find acceptance, as Ranade showed from an analysis of the position, as revealed by the Reform Societies' reports, how futile, owing to the variety of opinion, such a procedure would be. Tilak's attitude stiffened into one of hostility. He strongly criticised the Social Conference in a letter published in the *Bombay Gazette*—to which Ranade fully replied. He waged a wordy warfare against the reformers in his paper the *Kesari,* while Agarkar counter-attacked in his paper the *Sudharak.* "Tilak," his biographer tells us, "while emphatically not unfriendly to social reform, believed in the imperative necessity of checking, from the larger national standpoint, the disintegrating forces by fostering a due sense of pride in and respect for the social and religious institutions of the people. Mr. Tilak was for the blending of the old culture and the new. He strongly resented state interference for the simple reason that reform to be durable must be a growth from within. Mr. Tilak was gradually convinced of the futility of social reform as it was then propagated and was for the above reason compelled to adopt first an attitude of constructive opposition and then of neutrality."

We can gather the lines of Ranade's answer to Tilak's position from his lecture on "State Legislation in Social Matters" which was delivered in the year 1885:

"The State in its collective capacity represents the power, the wisdom, the mercy and charity, of its best citizens. What a single man, or a combination of men, can best do on their own account that the State may not do, but it cannot shirk its duty if it sees its way to remedy evils, which no private combination of men can check adequately or which it can deal with more speedily and effectively than any private combination of men can do."[17]

With regard to the fact that the Government in India was a foreign one, Ranade admitted that jealousy of foreign interference in social matters is not a bad sign, and said that if the interference were of foreign initiation the argument against it would be irresistible. But he says,

"The initiation is to be our own, and based chiefly upon the example of our venerated past, and dictated by the sense of the most representative and enlightened men in the community, and all that is sought at the hands of the foreigners is to give to this responsible sense, as embodied in the practices and usages of the respectable classes, the force and the sanction of law."[18]

Ranade admits, too, that there is reason in the contention that institutions, like constitutions, must grow and cannot be made to conform with foreign ideals to order. But he insists that,

"The change is sought not as an innovation, but as a return and restoration to the days of our past history. Those who advocate it, justify it on the authority of texts revered, and admitted to be binding to this day. The intermediate corruption and degradation was not of the nation's seeking. It was forced upon it by the predominance of barbarous influences, and by the intolerance of ruthless conquerors. That force having ceased to be operative, we must now return to the old order of things, if we are to grow to our old proportions."

Again he urges that Hindu social affairs are at present regulated by very stringent written laws which are enforced by our Courts of Justice. "What is now proposed is to substitute the more ancient and righteous law for a later degenerate offshoot of that law, cancel the travesty of law which is condemned by all, at least more amenable to reason, and utilize the force of State sanction as a final support."

To the contention that the law should be made use of only for suppression of positive crimes, whereas the evils now sought to be remedied are not crimes, Ranade replies:

"In most cases enforced widowhood and disfigurement, destruction of home sanctity by polygamous connections, stupidity of baby marriages, are not impulsive acts (i.e. they have not even that excuse) they are done in cold blood, and they inflict life-long and undeserved misery on helpless victims, while the offenders suffer but little. But so far as their moral heinousness is concerned, they are inflictions of injustice without any redeeming features and the criminal responsibility of the nation is beyond all reprieve."[19]

At the beginning of 1891, the fight over the Age of Consent Bill was at white-heat, for it was then that the Bill came before the Supreme Legislative Council. Great meetings, for and against, were held at Bombay and Poona. There was fierce controversy regarding the words of the *Shastras* on the matter, Bhandarkar and Telang being the protagonists who sought to prove that the *Shastras* sanctioned the reform, and Tilak the protagonist for proving the opposite. The anti-reformers declared that the change would mean the destruction of true religion, and that the Government would be breaking its promise of religious neutrality if it enacted the new law. A meeting held by the reformers at the Kridabhuvan in Poona had to be hastily brought to an end because students pelted the platform with stones and bricks. During all these disturbed days, Ranade was on tour in the Nagar District, but at Ahmednagar he took the opportunity of speaking on the matter and of showing unambiguously that he heartily favoured increasing the minimum age of consent.

From Nagar he went to the Sholapur District where he contracted cholera and was at the gates of death. When he returned to Poona, after his recovery, the Age of Consent Bill had been passed into law.

The anti-reformers, expressed their feelings of disgust and resentment by means of mimic satire. They prepared a pretended corpse, dressing it with much ingenuity, with eggs in its mouth, a necklace of biscuits round its neck, a bottle of spirits on its breast and copies of the *Indu Prakash* and the *Sudharak* under its arms. Followed by a crowd of children and loafers, it was carried before the dwellings of the prominent reformers, where the slogan was raised that they and all the reformers in the world were dead. Finally, the "corpse" was carried away and flung into a *nullah*.

In 1890, Pandita Ramabai's Sarada Sadan (a resident school for Indian girls, especially widows) was transferred from Bombay to Poona. Its chief object was to provide an asylum for young widows. The money required had been collected by the Pandit in America. Ranade, who was in thorough sympathy with the object, attended a meeting at which Miss Hamlin, the Pandit's assistant, tried to stir up the support of the Poona folk. During the meeting Ranade's mind seems to have been much agitated as to what he should do. At the last moment he saw his path clear, and, just as the people were starting to leave the hall, he rose to his feet and said that there and then they must set up a body to carry on this Widow's Home, otherwise they would be failing in their duty. As a result of the short but forceful speech that he made, about 40 persons expressed their willingness to take part in the directing body. The *Kesari* made much capital out of the fact that the Pandita was a Christian, and urged that it was not right to give the education of Hindu women into her care. Ranade's answer was that the fact about the teacher being a Christian was irrelevant, especially as it had been agreed upon that the school would be strictly secular in its character. The important point, Ranade said, was not the Pandita's religion, but the usefulness of her institution, and the advantages that through it would be enjoyed by friendless Hindu widows. Later on, however, when it became evident that some of the inmates of the institution were being strangely attracted towards Christianity by the Pandita's personal character, Ranade and his friends—in 1893—publicly disowned all connection with the institution. Ranade started a plan for the establishment of another Sadan, and got the length of publishing a notice in the papers regarding his intention, but the plan did not mature.

On 4th October, 1890, took place the famous Missionary Tea at the Panch Howds Mission. Fifty-two Brahman gentlemen including Ranade, were present on that occasion. In the course of the evening, the ladies of the Mission served tea and biscuits for the guests, and many of the Brahmans partook of the refreshment offered to them. Ranade himself did not touch the biscuits, nor did he put the cup to his lips, but in order not to show disrespect to his hostesses, he took a cup in his hands and, later on, put it down on a table.

Nothing happened until six months after. Then a certain rapid anti-reformer published in the *Vaibhava* an exact account of what had taken place at the Tea, and followed up that shortly afterwards with an account of a dinner at which three Non-Brahmans were present which Ranade had given in honour of a friend who had recently returned from a visit to Europe. Under this stimulus, the orthodox leaders at Poona brought the social pressure of excommunication to bear upon those who had participated in the Missionary Tea, and also upon priests, cooks, and water-carriers who kept up relations with the offenders. They were thus able to make things very unpleasant. When ceremonial days came round, and when the time came for thread-investiture or marriages, the excommunicated families could get no official Brahman to perform the required rites. This caused much mental pain, especially among the women-folk. Ranade did what he could to get Shastris and Brahmans who were attached to himself to carry out the ceremonies, but still the perplexity continued, and most of the people had not the patience and courage to follow his advice of quietly enduring the inconvenience until more enlightened days came round. It, therefore, became clear to Ranade that if he persisted in opposition to the authorities in this matter, considerable numbers would drop out of the reform movement.

Meanwhile, the matter had been brought before the Sankaracharya, and when he had been given to understand that Ranade and the others would bow to his decision, then, at the beginning of 1892, he sent down two Shastris to act as arbitrators. Ranade let it be known that his party would not decline to accept a penance which was compatible with self-respect, but that they would have nothing to do with any penance that aimed at degradation and public scron. After hearing the matter, the Sastris decided that on the performance of a mild penance—the payment of small money presents to Brahmanical priest, the excommunicated persons should be reinstated in the Brahman community.

Ranade himself felt no urgent need or desire for such reinstatement, for his own family peace had not been disturbed by his excommunication. He knew, however, that the peace of others had been deeply disturbed, and he therefore proposed that the acceptance or refusal of the terms of reinstatement should be a matter for the individual, and be settled according to the needs of the individual's position. But many of his friends felt strongly that it would not be fitting for them to take the penance if Ranade did not do so also. He, therefore, finally decided to make the required appeasement, and on 15th May, 1892, he went from Lonavla to Poona and performed the penance.

For a month afterwards Indian and Anglo-Indian newspapers poured criticism upon Ranade's conduct. It was asserted that his love for the people had waned, that his youthful courage had departed, that he had crushed the social reform movement, etc. Ranade defended his action in a letter that he sent to the *Bombay Gazette*, and in a lecture on "Mental Prepossessions" which he delivered on 5th June, 1892. In that lecture he pointed out that ever since the Age of Consent Bill controversy, the enemies of social reform had been on the look-out for some stick with which to beat the reformers and had found it in the *Panch Howds* affair. The anti-reformers wanted to use the tea-party incident in such a way as to make the masses think that the breaking of caste, by eating and drinking with people of other religions, was a chief point in the social reform movement. Seeing that if this idea were to gain currency, there was a probability of the whole reform movement collapsing, Ranade and his friends did not disregard the authority of the Sankaracharya. Here then we get the reason why Ranade sanctioned the doing of the penance. To have refused would probably have led to a big secession from the social reform ranks, and that for a reason which was not essential—for eating and drinking with men of other religions was no part of Ranade's social reform programme. If such caste-breaking intercourse by chance took place, then he saw no harm in accepting a penance which was in accordance with the *Sastras*, in order to put matters right. The reason why he himself took it, and also sanctioned for his followers who desired to undergo penance, was his unselfish consideration for his friends. He saw that refusal to do it himself would lead to continued trouble and unhappiness in the families of many of his followers who would not take the penance if their leader did not. Unselfishness, as Mr. Phatak points out, often receives the compensation of popular credit. But Ranade's unselfishness in this case resulted inevitably in public discredit, and yet having resolved what he ought to do, he faced the consequences with quiet unconcern.[20] Even his wife misunderstood him at the time, and for two or three days felt that he had made a big mistake. In an interesting passage in her *Reminiscences,* she writes how bitter her thoughts were when he went off to do the penance. Why should he go and involve himself in that disgrace, why not leave it to those whose lives were rendered troublesome by the excommunication? When Ranade returned by the evening train, she deliberately avoided going near him. However, when she saw him engrossed in his mail and newspaper, as if nothing unusual had occurred, she beheld him. Having made up his mind about a certain issue, he did it and his mind was at peace. Bitter and violent criticisms by his enemies or even friends could never break his calm serenity.[21]

Ranade's conduct in connection with the sequel to the Missionary Tea offers a wide field for reflection. Was he right to sanction the penance and to take it himself, or by giving way to prejudice instead of unbendingly opposing it, was he not, as John Morley puts it, in effect saying, "I cannot persuade you to accept my truth, therefore, I will pretend to accept your falsehood." In coming to a conclusion on this point we must give full weight to the fact that Ranade was consciously averse to the method of rebellion. We must remember that he was like a general in a campaign, seeking to lead to victory through a hostile country the small, ill-organised, and poorly disciplined army of Reform. Western education introduced about fifty years before had opened the eyes of Indians to glaring defects in their social institutions. The early generations of English-educated Indians accepted with unbounded admiration Western ideas and ways of life, and with undiscriminating scorn renounced the old Indian ways. But Western education touched only a mere fringe of the population, and those whom it did not touch were shocked and horrified by these new ways. Gradually the instinct of self-preservation and the pride of race asserted itself, and the pendulum swung to the opposite extreme. In the reaction all attempt at reform came to be opposed as unpatriotic and irreligious. Those who had the courage to speak out against the social evils were subjected to harassment and persecution. The very word "reformer" came to bear for the great majority of Indians a meaning that was evil. It looked as if the cause of social reform was doomed. It was Ranade who saved it.

"For 20 or 30 years," writes Mr. Patwardhan, "he was practically the life-breath of the reform movement. He organised the movement, focused the various forces and spasmodic activities of individual reformers; he shaped it anew, and reconciling it with the past, soldered it with all that was noble and precious in our heritage. He established a continuity where all seemed to be broken up and confused. Licence was over and its place was taken by chastened liberty. Revolution yielded place to evolution. Disruption ceased and a process of slow organic growth set in. He secured the health and well-being of the spirit of reform and was content to let alone the form it manifested itself in."[22]

Ranade himself once, in a letter written to Telang, said, "There are some matters in which we must stand out, but there is no reason why we should stand out on all matters simply for the fun of the thing." And perhaps the matter of the penance might be left at that—regarded as a point which in view of all the circumstances the mind of the strategist deemed it advisable to concede. One cannot but feel, however, that the concession was the outcome of a certain tenderness or lack of iron in Ranade's character, and that it was not merely a cool-headed move in a game. Sincerely and eagerly zealous of reform, he was at the same time temperamentally averse to self-assertion and revolt. He strove unweariedly to reach a lofty goal, but always by that path which seemed to involve the minimum of friction. His heart burned with sympathy for the Indian widow, and he laboured incessantly to improve her lot, but he could not bring himself to lay on the altar of that high cause, his filial obedience and his family's peace. Though a great reformer, he had not that adamantine nature which, esteeming the present travail as of no account, breathes an exalted, if stern, "amen" to the fateful necessity expressed in the words, "He that loveth father or mother more than me is not worthy of me." Ranade was too fundamentally cautious and had not in him enough of the spirit of pugnacity to make him adopt Gandhi's dictum that "a reformer's business is to make the impossible possible by giving an ocular demonstration of the possibility in his own conduct."[23] Nevertheless, his service to social reform in India was immense, and was such as probably only a man of his type could have rendered. Wisdom is justified of her children.

A circular letter signed by Ranade, Satyendranath Tagore, Lalshankar Umiyashankar, and a number of eminent men from all over India with a questionnaire as an accompaniment, was published along with the report of the eighth session of the Social Conference at Madras in 1894. The letter stated, *inter alia*: "Under the vivifying influences that are at present at work, India is regaining, however slowly, a national consciousness and life. Efforts are being made to strengthen social union, to interpret social usages in their true sense and to remove unnecessary and inconvenient restrictions. These are favourable indications. Our social organisation is not without its good features and they are not few; but there are also certain matters in which reform is urgently needed. Old bonds are losing their hold on the public mind. Such of them which are congenial to the healthy growth of our society need to be strengthened, and new ones substituted in place of those that do not suit the changed circumstances of our country. But no real progress in social matters is possible without public sympathy and earnest co-operation. With a view, therefore, to securing such sympathy and co-operation, it is desirable to ascertain the attitude of the intelligent portion of the community about the more important questions which affect vital social interests. Some of these questions have already engaged the attention of the Social Conference and other associations in the country. We have thought it fit to send the accompanying questions in the hope that you will be good enough to favour us with your opinion on the points raised therein and endeavour to obtain and send to us the written opinions of your friends whom you may consult on these questions. You need answer only of such questions as you may choose for yourself. It is proposed to compile and publish the opinions thus collected with a view to enlightening public opinion and to directing our particular efforts to those reforms which may be generally approved of. Such a compilation will, it is hoped, be of some help to the Social Conference and the several associations that have been taking great interest in social questions."[24]

The following 32 items were tackled in the form of questions. How many replies were received and whether any publication based on the replies saw the light of day is not known. But very probably the response was poor since no reference response to the circular letter and the questionnaire is met with in the subsequent annual addresses of Ranade. The questions, however, serve to show what ideas and objectives were engaging the minds of the leaders of the Social Conference in those days. Here are the questions:[25]

(1) *Female Education:* Female education is not progressing as rapidly as it ought to. Are there any special reasons in your province for such a state of things? If so, state them. What steps in your opinion are needed to carry on this work with more vigour? If you think that the present course of studies is not suited, what course would you recommend for girls? Are you and others in your town prepared to help pecuniarily or otherwise for spread of female education on the lines that you may suggest? What system of female education in your opinion would be popular and meet the requirements of our family life and surroundings?

(2) *Prohibition of the Use of Spirits and Intoxicating Drugs:* Which intoxicating drugs are in more general use in your province? What remedies may be adopted to check their use? Will the people in your town agree to co-operate in a movement for asking the authorities to remove from the heart of towns the shops for the sale of spirits and other intoxicating drugs? Would not the location of such shops outside the limits of towns do some good? In the case of classes which are more particularly addicted to the use of intoxicating drugs and drinks, would it not be possible to do something through the spiritual and caste leaders of those communities to check the evil?

(3) *Religious Disputes Between Hindus and Mahomedans*: In what places in your province have there been religious disputes between Hindus and Mahomedans? What were these due to? If you are aware of any respective rights of the two communities as regards public processions in your province, state them. Would it not be possible for the leaders of the two communities in your town to form a committee with a view to fixing the customary usage and to settle the disputes amicably when they arise, and keep up the good feeling between them both? If so, state if such leaders are willing to form a committee of conciliation.

(4) *Intercommunion in Food and Intermarriage*: What sub-divisions of your caste allow intercommunion in food at present? Do you think that intermarriage between such sub-divisions would be greatly beneficial to both? If so, would not the more intelligent men in your province be prepared to actively co-operate in bringing about the desired object?

(5) *Prostitutes and Dancing Girls*: (a) At present the houses of prostitutes are situated in the heart of towns. Do you not think that this is dangerous to public morals? What remedies would you propose to check the evil? (b) It is not unusual among some of our rich people to have nautch girls on occasions of religious ceremonies such as

marriage, thread-ceremony etc. How far is this practice salutary, and if any evils result from it, how will you check them?

(6) *High-Caste Child Widows*: Considering the pitiable condition of our high-caste child-widows, (a) would it not be desirable to allow them to re-marry? If you think that they may be allowed to do so under certain restrictions, what restrictions, in your opinion, are necessary to ensure the sympathy of the people? (b) How far is the public in your place prepared to allow the remarriage of such child-widows before puberty? (c) In what castes is the custom of disfiguring widows prevalent in your province? Is it not generally looked upon with disfavour? If so, ascertain how far people are ready to co-operate in discouraging the custom?

(7) *Sea-Voyage to Distant Countries*: Do you not think that the time has come to remove all social impediments in the way of those persons who go to foreign countries for education, trade or similar other purposes, and are you not of the opinion that these persons should be freely re-admitted into their caste? If you and others think some conditions should be imposed to conciliate caste feelings what are the minimum conditions, which people in your parts are prepared to impose?

(8) *Custom of Employing Hired Mourners*: Do you not consider that the custom of employing hired mourners prevailing among certain classes should be condemned altogether? So also would you not like to discourage the practice of crying loudly in public streets, when a funeral procession is passing?

(9) *Panchayats:* In how many villages that you have seen have you noted the ruinous effects of mutual animosities fomented by factions? If you have found any in your district, will the people of your place be prepared to assist the people of such villages in establishing Panchayats for amicably settling such disputes? If there are any difficulties in the way, what are they? How could they be removed?

(10) *Early Marriage and Extravagant Marriage and Funeral Expenses*:

(a) Many people at present marry improvidently and spend large sums beyond their means on marriage. By reason of the inability of parents to support themselves and their children, general impoverishment results and rich families are reduced to beggary. Is it not desirable that this state of things should be checked? If so, what remedies would you propose to check the evil? Would not the people in your province be prepared to discourage such improvident marriages by withholding aid, pecuniary or otherwise, and refusing to attend the celebration of such marriages?

(b) If a rule be made that boys should, in no case, be married before they have completed the age of 16 and girls before 10, would not the people in your province observe the same?

(c) Some people marry a second wife while the first is living. Do you not think that some restrictions are necessary in such a case? If so, what restrictions should be imposed?

(d) Some men marry girls of tender age, though they themselves are far advanced in age. Is it not necessary to condemn such marriages? Will people in your district have any objection to a prohibition of the marriage by old men after they have passed the age of 45 or 50?

(e) Is not the practice of receiving money as consideration for giving daughters in marriage condemned in your caste or province? Would not the people in your district exert themselves to oppose it?

(f) Are not *Hunda* demands now growing beyond reasonable limits? Is it not desirable to put some limits on such demands? What limit would you propose? Will it not be more beneficial to stop the practice of paying Hunda and introduce instead of it the system of investing the amount in the name of the bride in some safe security?

(g) Do your caste people spend extravagantly on marriages? If so, in what particular respects are they extravagant? In what particulars can the expenditure be curtailed?

(h) Do people in your province spend large sums of money in giving caste dinners in memory of or after the death of a relative? Do you not think that there is much room for reform in this matter also, without hurting the feelings of the parties concerned?

In respect of all these points how far can caste Panchayats be utilised to enforce rules made by them? If Panchayats cannot be so utilised, what other associations would you suggest?

(11) *Clubs*: At present clubs are established in several places. If you think that improvements are needed in these, what should they be? Is it not desirable to increase their number? What practical steps do you propose for making these institutions more popular and useful?

(12) *Competent Midwives and Nurses*: Have you not observed that the want of skilful midwives and nurses is much felt? If widows or other women were trained for the profession of midwives and nurses, would not people of your district avail themselves of their assistance? If any such women be prepared to learn the profession, will not people assist them pecuniarily?

(13) *National Education*: Large numbers of children are at present unable to avail themselves of the benefits of education by reason of the poverty and ignorance of their parents or other causes. Do you not think it necessary that every child should receive elementary education at least for four or five years? What steps should in your opinion be adopted to secure this object? Government may perhaps be moved to help us in this matter, but will the people be prepared to help themselves? Could the current of our charities be diverted to this object? If so, what steps do you think should be taken for the purpose?

If you think that there are difficulties in the way of introducing the system of national education in your province, what are those difficulties? What remedies, if any, suggest themselves to you for removing them?

(14) *School-buildings and Play-Grounds*: Do you not think that at least in large villages and towns every school should have a building of its own, and that a play ground should be attached to it? Government will probably assist in this matter, but will the people come forward to do so considering it as a proper object of charity?

(15) *Boarding Schools*: Several people have to send their sons to large towns for education. But there being no proper provision for their boarding and lodging, many boys are put to great inconvenience, and some of them go astray. Under these circumstances don't you think that some suitable provision is necessary with respect to boarding, lodging and proper control of these students in large towns? If boarding-houses were established, would the people of your district help pecuniarily? What arrangements would you like to have in the boarding-houses that have been established already or that may be established hereafter?

(16) *Kindergarten System*: Is it not now desirable to adopt the Kindergarten system for imparting education to small children with a view to making the education of children more popular? If you think that there are some drawbacks in the system or some difficulty in the way of introducing it, what are they? How can they be removed?

(17) *Education of Backward Classes*: Do you not think that some special provision should be made for the instruction of classes which are backward in education? What provision do you propose for your district? Could the current of our charities be turned in this direction also?

(18) *Education of Poor children*: Many poor children, who are intelligent and promising, are at present compelled to abandon their course of study for want of suitable means. Don't you think that the nation loses the benefit of their

talents? Would the people of your district raise a fund for assisting such students? If so, what scheme do you propose for the management of the fund? What should be the conditions on which alone pecuniary help is to be given?

(19) *Libraries and Gymnasia*: Is it not necessary at present to provide greater facilities to the people for reading and physical exercise with a view to creating a taste for these? If you think that free libraries and gymnasia should be established at different places in your district until an interest in these is created among the people, would you and others in your town assist in establishing such libraries and gymnasia?

(20) *Home Education*: Do you not think that in the matter of home education our people appear rather indifferent? If so, can this state of things be improved?

(21) *Charitable Dispensaries*: Have you not observed that people in villages have to put up with great inconvenience for want of due provision for medical aid? If efforts were made to establish charitable dispensaries for providing European and native medicines, would not people in your district be ready to assist? If you are of the opinion that it is necessary to divert the course of charities in this direction, in what way can this be done?

(22) *Pinjrapoles*: Merchants and traders have established *Pinjrapoles* in various places for helpless cattle. If you think that some improvements are necessary in these, please state them. Just as these institutions are established for helpless dumb animals, is it practicable to have a similar charitable institution in your town for helpless human beings, who have become disabled by infirmities or age to earn their livelihood? If so, will the people in your district be willing to help in the matter? State if such an institution should be separate. Can the *Pinjrapole* authorities not be induced to include this relief in their charity?

(23) *Street Beggars and Mendicants*: It is a great question as to what should be done for our beggars and mendicants. It is a matter demanding serious consideration whether the existing state of things with regard to street-beggars and mendicants should be allowed to continue or whether some improvement should be made in it.

The first question to be decided is: are all the classes of street-beggars and mendicants worthy of our charity? If not, from which of them may our charity be withheld. Is it practicable in your town to prevent able-bodied men and women from begging from door to door and make some separate provision for them? If an institution like the *Pinjrapole* are established for the whole body of really helpless beggars and mendicants, would the people in your district approve of the project and assist in the matter? Do you not think that some special provision should be made for poor students, who actually live on alms while prosecuting their studies? If so, what kind of provision do you suggest? If you think that all able-bodied beggars should be made to work for their maintenance rather than be given free alms, what suitable employment could you find for them in your town?

(24) *Devasthans and Annasatras* (Religious endowments and free boarding houses): Are there any *Devasthans*, *Annasatras* or *Sadavartas* in your province, and at what place? Are they managed properly? If any are found to be mismanaged, what is the cause of mismanagement and what remedies would you suggest for their better management?

(25) *Kirtans and Purans*: *Kirtans* and *Purans* are to some extent very useful means for imparting religious and moral instruction, but do you not find that these institutions fail to serve the purpose for which they seem to be intended? To what do you attribute this? If you are of the opinion that some improvements are needed, in these institutions, what are they? Could you suggest means by which we

could meet the requirements of the times through their agency?

(26) *Dramatic Performances*: The real object of dramatic performances is not kept in view and they would appear to have become mere means of amusement. Could you suggest means to make this institution more useful? Would not the representation of our social evils by means of dramatic performances be effectual?

(27) *Shimga and Moharram*: Is it not desirable to discourage as much as possible the improper and objectionable ways in which Moharram and Shimga are celebrated by some of our people? If so, what remedies do you propose?

(28) *Holy Places*: Is the money spent at these places usefully spent? If not, in what places within your knowledge is the charity misdirected? If you have observed anywhere any misdirected expenditure, state details. How can it be curtailed without injuring the religious susceptibilities of the people? If there are any holy places in your district, please state if any efforts have been made to provide separate buildings for the accommodation of pilgrims and to establish religious and charitable institutions at any of the several places? If not, do you not think it desirable that efforts should be made in this direction? What kinds of religious and charitable institutions should, you think, be established and where? Are decent shelters provided on the spots reserved for the cremation of dead bodies?

(29) *District Conference*: Do you not think that the establishment of a conference in every zilla (district) to discuss social questions will be of great use? If so, will not the people of your district be willing to hold such a conference once a year?

(30) *Itinerant Lectures*: Will the people of your province be prepared to make due provision for the expense of itinerant lecturers to explain to the masses such of the social reforms as may be approved of and found to need immediate action?

(31) *Permanent Fund*: Do you not think it necessary to raise a permanent fund for the expenses required to do the needful in the matter of awakening public opinion on questions of social reform? What means do you propose for raising such a fund? Would the people divert the current of their charities towards the above object?

(32) *General*: If there be any other questions, besides the above, deserving immediate consideration, please state them and give your opinion about them.

Although Ranade favoured all these reforms, it must be remembered that what he emphasised was not this or that reform, but the spirit behind them as has been pointed out earlier. As he said in Madras in 1898: "The issue is not this or that particular reform about which people have so much controversy but the general spirit of purity, justice, equality, temperance and mercy which should be infused into our minds and which should illumine our hearts. Is it to be the spirit of justice, charity, mercy, toleration and appreciation of all, or is it to be exclusiveness, haughtiness, pride, cruelty and misery of all kinds? The choice lies with us and we may choose which we prefer."

REFERENCES

1. Gidumal, Dayaram, *The Status of Women in India* (Ahmedabad: Navajivan Publishing House), 1953, pp. 13-14.
2. Kellock, James, *Mahadev Govind Ranade, Patriot and Social Servant, op. cit.*, p. 74.
3. *Ibid.*, p. 75.
4. Paravate, T. V., *Mahadev Gobind Ranade, op. cit.*, p. 155.
5. *Ibid.*, p. 156.
6. Kellock, *James, Mahadev Govind Ranade, Patriot and Social Servant, op. cit.*, p. 77.
7. *Ibid.*, p. 79.
8. Chintamani, C. Y., *Indian Social Reforms*, Part II (Allahabad: Kitabistan), 1947, pp. 127-28.
9. *Ibid.*, p. 25.
10. *Ibid.*, p. 91.

11. Kellock, James, *Mahadev Govind Ranade Patriot and Social Servant, op. cit.*, p. 83.
12. Chintamani, C. Y., *Indian Social Reforms, op. cit.*, pp. 95-109.
13. Kellock, James, *Mahadev Govind Ranade, Patriot and Social Servant, op. cit.*, p. 84.
14. *Ibid.*, pp. 84-85.
15. Gidumal, Dayaram, *The Status of Women in India, op. cit.*
16. Kellock, James, *Mahadev Govind Ranade, Patriot and Social Servant, op. cit.*, p. 87.
17. Athalye, D. V., *The Life of Lokmanya Tilak* (Poona: Sadashiv Path), 1921, pp. 54-55.
18. Kellock, James, *Mahadev Govind Ranade, Patriot and Social Servant, op. cit.*, p. 89.
19. *Ibid.*, p. 93.
20. Ranade, Ramabai, *Amchya Ayushatil Kahil Athavani* (trnsl.) by Kusumavati Deshpande, Ranade His Wife's Reminiscences (New Delhi: Publications Division, Ministry of Information and Broadcasting), 1963, p. 107.
21. Kellock, James, *Mahadev Govind Ranade, Patriot and Social Servant, op. cit.*, pp. 95-96.
22. *Young India*, 5th February 1925.
23. Paravate, T. V., *Mahadev Gobind Ranade, op. cit.*, pp. 157-159.
24. *Ibid.*, pp. 157-165.
25. *Ibid.*, p. 105.

6

PHILOSOPHY OF HISTORY

Causes of Movements of History

Ranade undertook to write a History of the Marathas. With this in view he made a collection of material—a paper embodying the results of his researches being afterwards published under the title, *Gleanings from the Maratha Chronicles*. Ranade went on to carry out the project all by himself. However, death prevented him from completely fulfilling the purpose. We have from his pen the first volume of the work, entitled *The Rise of the Maratha Power*, which was published in 1900. In this book Ranade controverts the widely held theory that the rise of the Marathas was little more than the outbursting of the "turbulent predatory spirit of the Hindus of Maharashtra," which had been smothered for a time but broke out when the chance offered itself through the contentions among the Muhammadan conquerors—a theory which makes History a haphazard chaos, devoid of moral interest. As against that view, Ranade seeks to show that in the Maratha history the deep and persistent laws of moral cause and effect were powerfully and constantly at work. He shows, for example, what a great part was played in the evolution of events by the "saints and prophets of Maharashtra." The religious movement of which they were the instruments "tended to raise the nation generally to a higher level of capacity both of thought and action, and prepared it, in a way no other nation in India was prepared, to take the lead in reestablishing a united native power in the place of foreign domination."[1]

More than half the book deals with the career of Shivaji, Robert the Bruce of Maratha history. Ranade makes clear the greatness of Shivaji not only as a warrior but also as a statesman and organiser—a point which previous historians had apparently tended to ignore. His summing up of the man who founded the Power from which the rule of India passed to the British is as follows:

"Religious fervour, almost at white heat, bordering on the verge of self-abnegation, a daring and adventurous spirit born of a confidence that a higher power than man's protected him and his work, the magnetism of superior genius which binds men together and leads them to victory, a rare insight into the needs of the times, and a steadfastness of purpose which no adverse turn of fortune could conquer, a readiness and resourcefulness rarely met with either in European or Indian history, true patriotism which was far in advance of the times, and a sense of justice tempered with mercy—these were the sources of the strength that enabled Shivaji to sow the seeds of a power which accomplished in the hands of his successors all that he had planned out, and enabled his race to write a chapter in Indian history to some purpose."[2]

In February 1899, Ranade wrote an essay on the *Mints and Coins of the Maratha Period;* and in June 1900, he wrote two papers called *Introduction to the Satara Raja's* and *Peshwa's Diaries.* In the latter we see how Ranade rejoiced in the thought that since the old Records at Poona had now been made available, it would be possible to write a history of the people of Maharashtra which would not be merely a narration of political events, but also "the condition of the people, how they lived and thrived, the pleasures which amused them, their superstitions and their beliefs, their morals, their manners and their customs." He declared that the material contained in these State Diaries which were kept by responsible officers in the Peshwa's Record Office, "shed a flood of light upon the real movements and the hopes and fears, the strength and weakness of the people for over a century, and for purposes of instruction and guidance, they far outweigh in value the narratives of wars and conquests, dynastic changes, and revolutions, which take up so much space in our ordinary histories."[3]

History has been described as the study of change in human society. What, in Ranade's opinion, was the underlying principle of change which occurs in the life of a civilisation, analogous to the 'dialectic' principle of Hegel and 'Challenge-and-response' of Toynbee?

Ranade does not point out any single principle underlying all changes in society. Nevertheless, he seems to be groping towards a view that moral vitality of a community is that single principle.

Increase or decrease in vitality causes changes for the better or the worse. Civilisation, can never be stationary; it must always be changing, either in the direction of progress or regress. Likening society to an organism, he says, " It is not possible for a living being, be the unit an individual or a collection of individuals, to remain stationary at any stage of progress achieved by them for any considerable time without, in fact, undergoing the slow process of decay and degradation."[4] So when a civilisation appears to be stationary, it is a sign that it is decaying. Further he seems to hold that this process of change is a struggle between the numerous elements of that civilisation. He does not say so, but it is implied in his observation, that, "When decay and corruption set in, it is not the fittest and the strongest that survive in the conflict of dead with living matter, but the healthy parts give way, and their place is taken up by all that is indicative of the fact that corruption has set in, and the vital force extinguished."[5] By implication he also seems to say that when regeneration begins, the fittest and the strongest elements of civilisation triumph over the rotten ones. From what follows these remarks, he seems to mean by 'elements', social customs, or usages. "If we stimulate the stiffed seeds of health and growth, and lop off dead excrescences, decay may yet be arrested."[6] But the struggling elements of civilisation may also be interpreted as different sides of the life of a community, social, political and economic; for, he elsewhere holds that a nation cannot make advance in one sphere while remaining backward in another.

The Idea of Progress

Do the changes in humanity which we call history lead to its betterment, so that humanity advances to something better? In other words, does humanity make progress? The theory of human progress was part of the intellectual climate of his day, and Ranade did believe in it. "Our new teachers must know how to introduce their pupils to a correct appreciation of the forces which are at work in the wider world outside and which, in spite of temporary checks or seeming reverses, represent all that is best in human efforts for the elevation and happiness of man."[7]

But Ranade's theory of progress had some distinct characteristics. In the first place, he was somewhat hesitant in his acceptance of this theory. He mentions the achievements of the modern times in the intellectual and industrial fields not to urge greater achievements, but only to appeal to his own countrymen to profit from them. Ranade treated the idea of progress rather casually, taking it for granted but not caring to examine or expatiate on it. But his Western contemporaries, like Spencer, not only realised its immense significance but were glowing with optimism about the future of humanity; and this note of exhilaration is missing in Ranade's writings. There were several reasons which account for the lukewarm attitude of Ranade towards this theory. A favourable circumstance for the acceptance of the idea of progress is that contemporary men should believe themselves to be unquestionably superior to those of ancient times;[8] and although the situation in the world in the latter half of the nineteenth century justified such a belief, Ranade, citizen of a degenerate country, could not feel that the achievements of modern science and technology were his as much as of the Westerners. For him, inferiority of contemporary India was as much real as the superiority of the contemporary world. He, therefore, could not feel the superiority of his age over the ancient times. Secondly, he could not subscribe to the view that the modern, Western civilisation was superior to the ancient Indian in every respect; see, for instance, his remark in an article in 1882: "The Science of the West has no doubt exploded popular superstitions and physical errors, but the philosophy of religion, and the religious yearning, stand as untouched as ever, as truth always does through all revolutions of thought."[9] Thirdly, though Ranade was fascinated by the achievements of Western civilisation, he was actually breathing the atmosphere of a civilization which had fallen, and he might have argued to himself as Hume did: "In several countries, the sciences and arts flourished, but they have also decayed. When they reached the highest perfection among one people, the neighbouring people were perhaps wholly unacquainted with them. It is uncertain therefore whether at present man is advancing or declining."[10] Ranade did not express this view, but it is most natural that, placed in a country which lay prostrate, this view should occur to him.

This lukewarm attitude towards the idea of progress is illustrated by the second characteristic of Ranade's view of this theory. To Ranade, retrogression is as important a phenomenon as progress. All advocates of the theory of progress note that humanity is not continuous, and that there are epochs of retrogression. These periods are explained away as being of less importance (e.g. by Turgot), or as necessary for further advance by Priestley who observes that they help the subsequent advances of knowledge by 'breaking the progress of authority', or as accompanied by a simultaneous though inconspicuous progress in other spheres (e.g., Turgot).[11] But Ranade, without denying progress or social evolution, feels greatly concerned with retrogression or devolution which also is a phenomenon of human history. He says, "The theory of evolution has, in this country to be studied in its other aspect of what may conveniently be called devolution." "One of the penalties of (an) arrest civilization is that, while stopping further growth, the seeds of decay and death are sown in the paralysed social organism. The 'Stationary East' is one of those popular fallacies which die a hard death, though killed and exploded a hundred times. It is not possible for a living being, be the unit an individual or a collection of individuals, to remain stationary at any stage of progress achieved by them for any considerable time without undergoing the slow progress of decay and degradation ..." Ranade's feeling of concern at degeneration leads him to undertake a "historical survey of the changes which have taken place during centuries of arrested growth in the social usages regulating the institution of marriage in the Aryan population of this country."[12]

The third characteristic of Ranade's view of progress is his emphasis on the moral aspect. Among Western thinkers the theory

of progress began as a theory of progress of knowledge, and it afterwards expanded into a general theory of human progress. Social fife, in man makes progress, includes several phenomena, and in the course of social progress the sum of man's physical, moral, intellectual, political and material life attains development. Western writers, in depicting and discussing progress, laid stress on intellectual development or progress of knowledge, and material progress which it promoted in the nineteenth century. To Ranade, however, the essence of progress was progress in the sphere of religion and morality. This emphasis on religious and moral aspect follows from his view that the essence of life is religion. Defending the religious attitude, he says, "There are those among us who ... will have us turn to more useful pursuits, which will secure for us the comforts, of this world, as the world understands comforts. Now, if there has been any feature of our national history which has been its glory and its reward for much suffering, it is the firm belief that 'not what a man hath, but what a man is, or can become', constitutes his real wealth. This is the protest which Indian thought has raised from all time, and which it will continue to raise to the end of time. The contrary view also derives no support from the highest Christian or European ideals before us. The whole mission of Christianity and civilisation is meaningless for those who read in it nothing but the progress of physical comforts, and the means of realising them."[13] Ranade worked for reform in all spheres—political, economic, social and religious—but social reform which he considered more important than the political had a moral and spiritual import. "The social evolution (i.e. social reform) must take place side by side, if it should not precede, the political growth that we desire to achieve. What is it, some of you will ask, that you require us to do in this work of internal freedom (i.e. not political freedom from foreigners but social emancipation—Writer)? I should reply, the evolution that we should seek in a change from constraint to freedom—constraint imposed by our own weaker nature over the freedom of our higher powers." He, therefore, is obviously delighted as he traces the progress of knowledge of religious truth in the course of human history, proudly pointing out that as India was the meeting place of religions, it was in India that the development of world's knowledge of religious

truth took place. "The great religions of the world took their birth here, and now they meet again as brothers prepared to welcome a higher dispensation, which will unite all and vivify all."[14] He shows how the rise of new sects like Buddhism and the impact of new religions like Mohammedanism have enriched the religious wisdom and raised the moral stature of the Indian people in the course of their long history. This is the only aspect of humanity's progress which Ranade has cared to trace in the clearest manner. It is a chance—Ranade called it Providence—that India was the theatre where this progress has taken place, presumably for all the world to see and learn from.

The fourth characteristic of Ranade's view of the idea of progress is that he refuted the notion, advanced by several interpreters of the theory, that oriental nations like India could not hope to progress. Some theorists of progress had propounded 'Laws of the Stages' in which they attributed the leadership of each stage to a particular country, the leadership of the last stage invariably being attributed to Western countries. Thus Condorcet distinguished the ten periods of civilisation in the history of Greek thought, the fifth is the history of Roman thought, and the latest is under the French Republic. Comte propounded the law of the stages, in which peoples pass on the torch to others as one stage is followed by another, and Egypt, Greece, Rome, Judea and France successively represented the stages in succession. Hegel regarded the history of the world as the progressive manifestation of the Spirit or God; and he conceived the Spirit as continuously moving from one nation to another in order to realise the successive stages of its self-consciousness. The third and the last stage is designated by Hegel as the Germanic world. The inference from these popular philosophies of history was that oriental nations could only be backward in the march of the world civilisation. Many understood this to mean that they must remain backward for ever. Ranade strongly protested against this view. He said, "Some of the wisest among them (Europeans) have demonstrated to their own satisfaction that all oriental races have had their day, and that nothing is now left to them but to vegetate and die, and make way for betters ... If these black forbodings were really inspired prophecies,

our outlook would be dark indeed. Happily for us these prophecies are not true, and what is more, it is in our power to falsify them. History does not countenance them, and the teachings of science are not in their favour."[15] He argues that the long history of India shows, not decay, but a gradual development, the nation to a higher ideal if not of actual facts, at least of potential capabilities; while science, which teaches that environments determine growth, shows that, under the new environments created by contact with Britain such as law and order and participation in the commerce of the world, India's growth may be hastened. This second argument deserves some notice. He was here relying on the doctrine of the possibility of indefinitely moulding the characters of men by laws, institutions and other elements of social environments, which doctrine laid the foundation of the theory of the perfectibility of humanity, and thus marked an important stage in the development of the idea of progress. It was first propounded by Turgot, who declared that human mind everywhere contains the germs of progress, and by Helvetius, who said that intellectual and moral inequalities between man and man arise entirely from differences in education and social circumstances, so that if you change education and social institutions, you can change the character of men. But these Encyclopaedists had deduced this theory of the malleability of human nature by education and institutions from the sensational psychology of Locke; and Ranade, a believer in innate ideas, could not have accepted this system of psychology.

The fifth characteristic was that in his idea of progress Ranade found room for God's Providence. This is of special interest because, as J.B. Bury says, "It was just the theory of an active Providence that the theory of Progress was to replace; and it was not till men felt independent of Providence that they could organise a theory of Progress."[16] Ranade reconciled the theories of Providence and Progress in two ways. First, in accepting the idea of Progress he does not accept the law of progress, the working of which is inescapable. All he says about this is that there are "forces which are at work in the wider world outside and which, in spite of temporary checks and seeming reverses, represent all that is best in human efforts for the elevation and happiness of man."[17] The

forces 'are at work', that is all. They are not inexorable; they have to face 'temporary checks and seeming reverses'. It is true that he speaks of 'the law eternal' standing 'above all mere ordinances and institutes', the law 'of justice and equality, of pity and compassion', and says, "We can no more resist the stream of these influences as working for righteousness than we can roll back the tide."[18] But this is the description of the law of Providence, not of the law of Progress. There is no 'law' of Progress; only, there are forces at work in its favour. Secondly, Ranade's 'Providence' is not active except through laws and human conscience. Pronouncing miracles or 'occasional breaches of the uniformities of nature,' as unnecessary and incredible, he says, "the continuance of the universe of matter in its ordained course, equipoised between all manner of distracting forces, is a greater standing miracle in favour of Theism than any number of violations of this uniform course ... " At one time in the intellectual history of Europe, Providence and Progress sharply opposed to each other that anyone believing in both would have been considered riding two horses at a time. Descartes affirmed the principle of the invariability of the laws of nature, or the immutability of the processes of nature, which collided with the theory of active Providence. For, only when, on the strength of this principle, men felt independent of Providence, they could organise a theory of Progress. The Deists, however, reconciled God and laws by holding that, "The function of the Deity was virtually confined to originating the machine of nature, which, once regulated, was set beyond any further interference on his part, though His existence might be unnecessary for its conservation." Ranade, like Western believers in God in his time who moved from Deism to Theism, thought of God also as immanent, informing and sustaining the universe, acting by law and through human conscience. Thus, by regarding Progress not as an unavoidable law but a force, Ranade leaves room for the influence of Providence; and by regarding Providence not as capriciously controlling the operations of nature and the affairs of men, but as acting only through uniformities or laws, Progress is allowed by Ranade to operate as a tendency of social life in which "man has a measure of free agency."[19]

Philosophy and History

Several writers who propounded philosophies of history established a relation between the movement of human history with their general philosophies. Ranade did not do so; but a student of his thought can construct such a relationship. Ranade's general philosophy can be briefly stated thus. Human mind cannot help seeking the understanding of the Universe. Underlying all thought of man on this subject, there are three postulates, the 'I', i.e. self or man the 'Non-I', i.e. matter or nature, and Supreme Existence which synthesises both. These three postulates of existence, man, nature and Supreme Existence, are distinct and yet harmonised together. Nature and man, each have definite relations of subordination to the great Infinite which rules over them and harmonises them. That Infinite, or God, is not a being among similar other beings setting the mechanism of the world in motion from outside; God is immanent in everything and overrules the Universe. God is not exhausted by the limits of his work, but is bigger than the Universe, encircling it and exceeding it on all sides. The precise relation existing between God and the creation is a mystery which transcends our knowledge; with our limited vision we are unable to unravel it. But there is no doubt that God shapes and regulates nature. Skilful design and kind disposition which are seen in the inanimate and animate world are strong evidence to show that He controls it for His purposes; for, order means reason, conscious mind, or personal will. Geology and Astronomy demonstrate how the physical world is ordered and has a development from imperfect to perfect, and from simple to the complex order of things. But God does not regulate nature from outside; he is immanent. The phrase 'God immanent in nature' signifies only the divine activity in regulating nature for the purposes of law and order, beauty and benevolence, power and wisdom. God regulates not only nature but also man. The distinguishing feature of man is his self-conscious reason and his volition, free to act or not to act, within certain well-defined limits. Man thus occupies a higher plane of being. How is this higher existence subordinated to the overruling Providence ? Man's spiritual relations with this universal Soul are made manifest by the sense of conscience in him, which makes him feel that he is responsible for the proper exercise of his delegated freedom. "He feels that the spirit immanent in the universe about him manifests His presence in him through this faculty of conscience." God is the moral Governor of the Universe. And " the whole scheme of God's government is intended to promote the growth of the Soul's capacities and perfect its powers."[20]

Such, in brief, is Ranade's general philosophy which he calls 'natural Theism'. From this philosophy, it is not impossible to construct a theory of the movement of human history. Such a theory includes four propositions. In the first place, it is not possible to know the divine plan, or God's Providence, in detail, because the precise relation between God and the created universe is a mystery beyond human comprehension. All that we know is that God regulates our affairs, and that the purposes he secures are law, order, beauty, benevolence and wisdom. In the second place: God's activity in regulating human history can never be through miracles or breaches of law; because law and order is one of the very purposes of God's Providence. God secures His purpose through the laws He has devised. In the third place, in human history, God secures His benevolent purposes through conscience of men; and this would be especially so through the medium of great men—men with highly developed conscience and with exceptional capacities, such as saints, prophets, statesmen and generals. Lastly, if a major event in human history conducive to man's happiness and moral elevation occurs by chance, it is correct to confer that the event is according to the Providence of God. Speaking of Muslim rule over India, he says, "It cannot be easily assumed that in God's Providence, such vast multitudes as those who inhabit India were placed, centuries together under influences and restraints of alien domination, unless such influences and restraints were calculated to do lasting service in the building up of the strength and character of the people in directions in which the Indian races were most deficient."[21] A major event, Providence, and benevolent influence must go together; if two of them are present, it is safe to infer that the third also is present. To say all this, however, is not to claim to know the scheme of Providence, because human mind is too frail to know it. What makes the major event Providential is, first, its benevolent nature and, second, inexplicability on any other ground. God has granted a certain amount of autonomy to man, whose actions, for this reason, are unpredictable; God also is in contact with human beings through, their conscience; if men in general, rather than choosing other courses of action, choose only the ones which ultimately lead to human welfare, they are acting according to God's desire. It is in this sense that unpredictable but beneficent events resulting from such unpredictable but good actions are due to the Providence of God. Such is the clarification of Ranade's conception of Providence in history. The conception is open to objections, but the objections need not be considered here.

A Generalisation from the History of India

A philosophy of history has been described as a form of historical synthesis.[22] If a certain synthesis is confined to the history of only a part of the universe, is it entitled to be called a philosophy of history? Comte had confined his review to European civilisation, and his synthesis cannot claim to be a synthesis of universal history; and yet he is considered to have propounded a philosophy of history. In one of his essays, Ranade reviewed the history of India and very nearly came to make a generalisation of such a profound character that it might almost be treated as a synthesis of the history of India. Be that as it may, it is interesting to notice that generalisation. It shows a wide sweep of induction. Moreover, it helps to explain some of his ideas on Indian politics.

In his "Introduction to Mr. Vaidya's Book", he surveys the rise and fall of women's rights and status in Hindu Aryan society from early Vedic times to his own day. In earliest times when Aryans were engaged in invasion and conquest, women's status was low. After they settled down, 'the necessities of war gave place to gentler virtues and victories of peace', and women were given a high status, in fact a status equal to men. This went on for several centuries. But after a time Aryans fell to fighting among themselves; murderous wars between Brahmins and Kshatriyas devastated the land. Under the pressure of these complicated difficulties, the strong love for active virtues of fighting and hunting developed; there arose a new philosophy which regarded life and being itself as a pain and a calamity, and woman, being weak, as a snare and a burden. Further deterioration occurred after a new development. "The down-trodden races, which had been driven to the hills, issued from their haunts, and fell upon the demoralised and disunited Aryan Kingdoms from all sides. At the same time, a new race of invaders from Central Asia, partly Scythian and partly Mongolian in stock, entered India by the north-west." "This process of upheaval of non-Aryan races and the invasion and settlement of barbarian Scythian conquerors was in active development for many centuries, and these ethnic and political forces have profoundly modified the institutions and usages of modern India. They brought to the surface races of men with a lower civilisation, more patriarchal, and therefore less chivalrous, ideals of life." Women's position sank low again, even lower than ever, as a result of the impact of the barbarians' customs and usages. Gradually the better and the Aryan portion of the community recovered from the surprise and the discomfiture, and the dark clouds began to clear up. "The Aryan religion, social polity, and marriage institutions reformed on a footing of compromise... This form of restoration and renaissance was again interrupted by the Mohammedan invasions, which repeated for some centuries all the horrors of the previous dark period." "It will be clear from this review that internal dissentions, the upheaval of non-Aryan and the predominance acquired by barbarous Scythian and Mohammedan conquerors, degraded the condition of the female sex...Political and ethnic agencies of great power have wrought the evil... Fortunately India now has before it the example of the British who are Aryans with purely Aryan customs unaffected by the customs of barbarians.[23]

The conclusion to which Ranade came is here put by him in a form which is not the form of a generalisation. If put in that form, it would be somewhat as follows: Whenever there is disorder, either due to internal dissensions or to foreign invasion, there is degradation, and whenever there is peace and order, there is gradual progress. If the barbarian races come to have an upper hand, the degradation is greater. Even with the barbarian predominance, if peace and order last for a long period, progress in civilisation is attained. If men of a superior civilisation invade and conquer, though the temporary disorder is inimical to progress, in settled times the rule of foreign superiors is conducive to progress. In short, peace and order are vital to progress, and next in importance, from this point of view, is the situation that the governing power should be either the indigenous power or a power whose civilisation is superior.

REFERENCES

1. Ranade, M.G., *Rise of the Maratha Power* (New Delhi: Publications Division, Ministry of Information and Broadcasting, Government of India), 1961, p. 172.
2. *Ibid.*
3. Kellock, James, *Mahadev Govind Ranade: Patriot and Social Servant, op. cit.*, p. 203.
4. Ranade, M.G., *Religious and Social Reforms, op. cit.*, p. 26.
5. *Ibid.*, p. 27.
6. *Ibid.*
7. Ranade, Ramabai, *Miscellaneous Writings of the Late Hon'ble Mr. Justice M.G. Ranade, op. cit.*, p. 246.
8. Bury, J.B., *The Idea of Progress* (London: Oxford University Press), 1960, p. 66.
9. Ranade, Ramabai, *Miscellaneous Writings of the Late Hon'ble Mr. Justice M.G. Ranade, op. cit.*, p. 287.
10. Bury, J.B., *The Idea of Progress*, op. cit., p. 219.
11. *Ibid.*, p. 156.
12. Ranade, M.G., *Religious and Social Reforms, op. cit.*, p. 27.
13. *Ibid.*, pp. 2-3.
14. Ranade, Ramabai, *Miscellaneous Writings of the Late Hon'ble Mr. Justice M.G. Ranade, op. cit.*, p. 126.
15. *Ibid.*, p. 115.
16. Bury, J.B., *The Idea of Progress, op. cit.*, p. 167.
17. Ranade, Ramabai, *Miscellaneous Writings of the Late Hon'ble Mr. Justice M.G. Ranade, op. cit.*, p. 246.
18. *Ibid.*, p. 234.
19. Ranade, M.G., *Religious and Social Reforms, op. cit.*, p. 268.
20. *Ibid.*, p. 267.
21. Ranade, Ramabai, *Miscellaneous Writings of the Late Hon'ble Mr. Justice M.G. Ranade, op. cit.*, pp. 219-20.
22. *Encyclopaedia of Social Sciences*, Vol. VII, p. 360
23. *Ibid.*, pp. 70-76.

BIBLIOGRAPHY

Athalye, D.V., *The Life of Lokmanya Tilak* (Poona: Sadashiv Path), 1921.

Banerji, Arun, *Finances in the Early Raj: Investments and the External Sector* (New Delhi: Sage Publications), 1995.

Black, R.D. *Collison, Economic Thought and the Irish Question, 1817-1870* (Cambridge: Cambridge University Press),1960.

Blaug, Mark, *Economic Theory in Retrospect* (Cambridge: Cambridge University Press), 1978.

Bury, J.B., *History of the Freedom of Thought* (London: Oxford University Press), 1960.

Bury, J.B., *The Idea of Progress* (London: Oxford University Press), 1960.

Chakravarty, S., "Drain Theory of Dadabhai Naoroji," a paper presented to the Indian Economic Association Conference, December 1968.

Chandra, Bipin, *Ranade's Economic Writings* (New Delhi: Gian Publishing House), 1990.

Chandra, Bipin, *The Rise and Growth of Economic Nationalism in India, Economic Policies of Indian National Leadership, 1880-1905* (New Delhi: People's Publishing House), 1966.

Charlesworth, Neil, *British Rule and the Indian Economy, 1800-1914* (London: Macmillan), 1982.

Chaudhuri, K.N., "India's International Economy in the Nineteenth Century: An Historical Survey", Modern Aśian Studies, Vol. 2, No.1 (January), 1968.

Chintamani, C.Y., *Indian Social Reforms*, Part II (Allahabad: Kitabistan), 1947.

Clark, Colin, *Conditions of Economic Progress* (London: MacMillan and Co. Ltd.), 1949.

Dantwala, M.L., *Poverty in India, Then and Now, 1870-1970* (Delhi: MacMillan), 1973.

Das, M.N., *Indian National Congress Versus the British,* Vol. 1 (1885-1918), Delhi, 1978.

Dasgupta, Ajit K., *A History of Indian Economic Thought* (London: Routledge), 1993.

Datta, Bhabatosh, *The Evolution of Economic Thinking in India* (Dr. P.N. Banerjea Memorial Lectures, 1961) (Calcutta: Federation Hall Society), 1962.

Dimand, Robert W., "I have no Great Faith in Political Arithmetic: Adam Smith and Quantitative Political Economy" in *Measurement, Quantification and Economic Analysis: Numeracy in Economics,* edited by Ingrid H. Rima (London: Routledge), 1995.

Dutt, Romesh, *The Economic History of India under the British Rule*, Vols. 1, 2 & 3 (New Delhi: Publications Division, Ministry of Information and Broadcasting, Government of India), 1963.

Gadgil, D.R., *Industrial Evolution of India* (Delhi: Oxford University Press), 1959.

Ganguli, B.N., *Indian Economic Thought: Nineteenth Century Perspectives* (New Delhi: Tata-McGraw Hill Publishing Co. Ltd.), 1978.

Georgescu-Roegen, Nicholas, *Analytical Economics: Issues and Problems* (Cambridge, Massachusetts: Harvard University Press), 1966.

Gidumal, Dayaram, *The Status of Women in India* (Ahmedabad: Navajivan Publishing House), 1953.

Gopalakrishnan, P.K., *Development of Economic Ideas in India, 1880-1914* (Gravenhange: Institute of Social Studies), 1954.

Green, T.H., *Principles of Political Obligations* (London: Allen and Unwin), 1934.

Gupta, Ajit Das, *A History of Indian Economic Thought* (Madras: T.R. Publications Private Limited), 1990.

Hallowell, G.H., *Modern Political Thought* (New York: Holt), 1953.

Jagirdar, P.J., *Mahadeo Govind Ranade* (New Delhi: Publications Division, Ministry of Information and Broadcasting, Government of India), 1971.

Jagirdar, P.J., *Studies in the Social Thought of M.G. Ranade* (New York: Asia Publishing House), 1963.

Javedkar, S.D., *Adhunik Bharat* (Pune: Sadashiv), 1947.

Jha, Shiva Chandra, *A History of Indian Economic Thought* (Calcutta: Firma K.L. Mukhopadhyay), 1981.

Kabir, Humayun, *The Indian Heritage* (Bombay: Bharatiya Vidya Bhawan), 1953.

Karmakar, A.D., *Economic Thought of Modern India* (Dharwar: J.S.S., Institute of Economic Research), 1974.

Karunakaran, K.P., *Indian Politics from Dadabhai Naoroji to Gandhi: A Study of the Political Ideas of Modern India* (New Delhi: Gitanjali Publishing House), 1988.

Kellock, James, *Mahadev Govind Ranade: Patriot and Social Servant* (New Delhi: Rupa & Co.), 2003.

Knight, Robert, India: *A Review of England's Financial Relations Therewith* (London: W.J. Johnson), 1968.

Lakatos, Imre, "Falsification and the Methodology of Scientific Research Programmes" in *Criticism and the Growth of Knowledge* edited by Imre Lakatos and Alan Musgrave (Cambridge: Cambridge University Press), 1970.

Lipton, Michael and Ravallion, Martin, "Poverty and Policy", Policy Research Working Papers, No. WPS 1130 (Washington: The World Bank), 1993.

Loganathan, *A History of Economic Thought* (New Delhi: S. Chand and Company Ltd.), 1987.

Madan, G.R., *Economic Thinking in India* (Madras: S. Chand & Co.), 1982.

Majumdar, Jatindra, Kumar (ed.), *Indian Speeches and Documents on British Rule, 1821-1918* (London), 1937.

Mankar, G.A., *A Sketch of the Life and Works of the Late Mr. Justice M.G. Ranade* (Bombay: Dayabhai), 1902, Vol. I.

Masani, R.P., *Builders of Modern India—Dadabhai Naoroji* (New Delhi: Publications Division, Ministry of Information and Broadcasting, Government of India), 1960.

Masani, R.P., *Dadabhai Naoroji: The Grand Old Man of India* (London: George Allen and Unwin Ltd.), 1939.

Marx, Karl and Fredrick, Engels, *On Colonialism* (Moscow: Progress Publishers), 1965.

Mukherjee, M., *National Income of India Trends and Structure* (Calcutta: Statistical Publishing Society), 1969.

Nabers, Lawrence, 'The Positive and Genetic Approaches' in *The Structure of Economic Science Essays on Methodology,* edited by Sherman Roy Krupp (Englewood Cliffs, N.J.: Prentice-Hall, Inc.), 1966.

Nanda, B.R., *Gokhale, Gandhi and the Nehru's Studies in Indian Nationalism* (London: George Allen and Unwin Ltd.), 1990.

Naoroji, Dadabhai, *Poverty and Un-British Rule in India* (New Delhi: Publications Division, Ministry of Information and Broadcasting, Government of India), 1962.

Naoroji, Dadabhai, *India's Wrongs and Remedy* (Madras: The Commonwealth Office), 1917.

Pandey, Shridhar, *Economic History of India* (Hindi) (Patna: Motilal Banarsidass), 1991.

Panikkar, K.M., *Asia and Western Dominance* (London: George Allen and Unwin), 1964.

Pound, Roscoe, *Spirit of Common Law* (New York: Yale University Press), 1955.

Sen, J.M., History of Elementary Education in India (Calcutta: Suptd., Government and Printing), 1917.

Parekh, C.L., *Essays, Speeches, Address and Writings (on Indian Politics) of the Hon'ble Dadabhai Naoroji* (Bombay: Asia Publishers), 1887.

Parliamentary Debates (House of Commons), Fourth Series, Vol. XI, 13th April 1893.

Paravate, T.V., *Mahadev Gobind Ranade* (Bombay: Asia Publishing House), 1963.

Patwardhan, R.P. (ed.), *Dadabhai Naoroji Correspondence, Child and Youth Section,* Vol. II, Part I (Bombay: Allied Publishers), 1977.

Patwardhan, W.B., "Justice M.G. Ranade and Social Reform in Western India," *Indian Interpreter*, January 1911.

Paul, R.R., *History of Economic Thought* (New Delhi: Kalyani Publishers), 1979.

Ranade, Ramabai, *Amchya Ayushatil Kahil Athavani* (trnsl.) by Kusumavati Deshpande, Ranade: His Wife's Reminiscences (New Delhi: Publications Division, Ministry of Information and Broadcasting), 1963.

Ranade, Mahadev Govind, *Ranade's Economic Writings* edited by Bipan Chandra (New Delhi: Gian Publishing House), 1990.

Ranade, M. G., *Religious and Social Reforms* (New Delhi: Sahitya Akademi), 1992.

Ranade, M.G., *Rise of the Maratha Pov'er* (New Delhi: Publications Division, Ministry of Information and Broadcasting, Government of India), 1961.

Ranade, Ramabai, *Miscellaneous Writings of the Late Hon'ble Mr. Justice M.G. Ranade* (New Delhi: Sahitya Akademi), 1992.

Rao, V.K.R.V., *An Essay on India's National Income, 1925-1929* (London: George Allen and Unwin), 1939.

Robinson, Joan, *An Essay on Marxian Economics* (London: Macmillan), 1966.

Schumpeter, J.A., *History of Economic Analysis* (New York: Oxford University Press), 1954.

Scweinitz Jr. Karl de, *The Rise and Fall of British India: Imperialism as Inequality* (London: Methuen & Co.), 1983.

Sen, R.K. and Mandal, S.K., "Ranade's Analysis of India's Population Problem and The Views of Naoroji and Doskar," I.E.A., 75th Conference Volume, 1992.

Sen, Sunanda, *Colonies and the Empire India, 1890-1914* (Hyderabad: Orient Longman), 1922.

Shanmugasundaram, V., *Indian Economic Thought and Policy* (New Delhi: S. Chand and Company Ltd.), 1981.

Singh, Gurumukh N., *Indian Constitutional and National Development* (Ajmer: Sachin), 1959.

Singh, V.B., *From Naoroji to Nehru* (New Delhi: MacMillan), 1975.

Speeches and Writings of Gopal Krishan Gokhale (Bombay: Asia Publishing House), 1962.

Stark, Werner, *The History of Economics in its Relation to Social Development* (London: Kegan Paul, Trench, Trubner & Co.), 1944.

Studenski, Paul, *The Income of Nations* (New York: New York University Press), 1958.

Viner, Jacob, *Studies in the Theory of International Trade* (London: George Allen and Unwin), 1960.

Watkins, F., *The Political Traditions of the West* (London: Nelson), 1953.

World Bank, *World Development Report, 1990* (Oxford: Oxford University Press), 1990.

Zaidi, Moin A., *Dadabhai Naoroji, Speeches and Writings* (New Delhi: Indian Institute of Applied Political Research), Vol. 1, 1985.

Index